Mark J. Larson

M000295742

To Win Our
Neighbors for Christ

Explorations in
Reformed Confessional Theology

Editors
Daniel R. Hyde and Mark Jones

To Win Our
Neighbors for Christ

The Missiology of the Three Forms of Unity

Wes Bredenhof

REFORMATION HERITAGE BOOKS
Grand Rapids, Michigan

To Win Our Neighbors for Christ
© 2015 by Wes Bredenhof

Reformation Heritage Books
2965 Leonard St. NE
Grand Rapids, MI 49525
616-977-0889 / Fax 616-285-3246
orders@heritagebooks.org
www.heritagebooks.org

Printed in the United States of America
15 16 17 18 19 20/10 9 8 7 6 5 4 3 2 1

Library of Congress Cataloging-in-Publication Data

Bredenhof, Wes.
  To win our neighbors for Christ : the missiology of the three forms of unity / Wes Bredenhof.
    pages cm. — (Explorations in Reformed confessional theology)
  Includes bibliographical references and index.
  ISBN 978-1-60178-375-2 (alk. paper)
  1. Reformed Church—Creeds. 2. Belgic Confession. 3. Heidelberger Katechismus. 4. Canons of Dort. 5. Missions. I. Title.
  BX9428.A1B74 2015
  238'.42—dc23
                              2014046831

For additional Reformed literature, request a free book list from Reformation Heritage Books at the above address.

Contents

Series Preface

The creeds of the ancient church and the doctrinal standards of the sixteenth- and seventeenth-century Reformed churches are rich theological documents. They summarize the essential teachings of Scripture, express biblical doctrines in meaningful and memorable ways, and offer pastoral guidance for the heads and hearts of God's people. Nevertheless, when twenty-first-century readers pick up these documents, certain points may be found confusing, misunderstood, or irrelevant for the church.

The Exploration in Reformed Confessional Theology series intends to clarify some of these confessional issues from four vantage points. First, it views confessional issues from the *textual* vantage point, exploring such things as variants, textual development, and the development of language within the documents themselves as well as within the context in which these documents were written. Second, this series views confessional issues from the *historical* vantage point, exploring social history and the history of ideas that shed light upon these issues. Third, this series views confessional issues from the *theological* vantage point, exploring the issues of intra- and inter-confessional theology both in the days these documents were written as well as our day. Fourth, this series views confessional issues from the *pastoral* vantage point, exploring the pressing pastoral needs of certain doctrines and the implications of any issues that cause difficulty in the confessions.

In exploring our vast and deep heritage in such a way, our ultimate goal is to "walk worthy of the Lord unto all pleasing, being fruitful in every good work, and increasing in the knowledge of God" (Col. 1:10).

—Daniel R. Hyde and Mark Jones

Author's Preface

The exercise is simple: Find the latest book introducing the study of Christian missions. If it mentions the history of missions, you can expect to read that the Protestant Reformation of the sixteenth century was a movement lacking missionary zeal. German mission scholars even coined a technical term for this alleged dearth of missionary enthusiasm: *missionslauheit* (missions-lukewarmness). Missiology can be defined as the science or study of mission in all its different aspects—it is an academic endeavor that has the task of delineating the what and how of mission. It has virtually become a given in this field that the Reformation was not oriented to the missionary task of the church, and this has been repeated so often that it has become a truism.

The claim appears to have been made first by Gustav Warneck in the nineteenth century.[1] It has since appeared in many other texts. For example, a missions textbook entitled *Introducing World Missions* claimed,

---

1. Gustav Warneck, *Outline of a History of Protestant Missions from the Reformation to the Present Time* (New York: Fleming H. Revel Company, 1901), 19.

"The Protestant Reformers Martin Luther, Huldrych Zwingli, and John Calvin said little about foreign mission. Believing that the world had been evangelized centuries before, they focused their energies on reforming Christian life within the Western church."[2] Similarly, Timothy Tennent's recent *Invitation to World Missions* claims that "the sixteenth century Protestant Reformation did not produce *any* missionaries."[3] This sweeping claim is easy to refute. Besides the hundreds of young men sent out to evangelize pseudo-Christian Europe, the Reformed church of Geneva sent out foreign missionaries to Brazil in 1556. These missionaries worked, albeit briefly, among the Tupinamba Indians.[4] First-generation Reformers such as William Farel and Anthony Saucier worked to bring the Waldensian movement into greater conformity with the biblical gospel.[5] Martin Bucer has been described as a "father of Reformed mission."[6] His writings are full of evidence of missionary fervor. More

2. A. Scott Moreau, Gary R. Corwin, and Gary B. McGee, *Introducing World Missions: A Biblical, Historical, and Practical Survey* (Grand Rapids: Baker, 2004), 120–21.

3. Timothy C. Tennent, *Invitation to World Missions: A Trinitarian Missiology for the Twenty-First Century* (Grand Rapids: Kregel, 2010), 248 (emphasis added).

4. Wes Bredenhof, "John Calvin and Missions," *Christian Renewal* 27, no. 11 (February 25, 2009), 24.

5. Giorgio Tourn et al., *You Are My Witnesses: The Waldensians across 800 Years* (Torino: Claudiana Editrice, 1989), 69–73.

6. L. J. Joosse, *Reformatie en zending, Bucer en Walaeus: vaders van reformatorische zending* (Goes: Oosterbaan & Le Cointre B.V., 1988).

examples could be mentioned.[7] Despite this, it is remarkable that missiologists continue to claim, for at least two related reasons, that the Reformation was deficient in regard to missions.

First, this claim has a long history. As mentioned above, my research reveals that it has been circulating since at least 1874, when missiologist Gustav Warneck (1834–1910) asserted it. With the passage of time, it has simply become an established "fact," even though just a cursory investigation reveals a different picture.

Second, this claim simply demonstrates the theological prejudice of the first ones to make it rather than being based on historical data. The first ones to make this claim, along with many others down the line, had little sympathy for the Reformation and its concerns.[8] Some even had an antipathy for the Reformation. With such an attitude, the Reformation was presented in mission history for *what it must have been* rather than for *what it really was*.

I intend to revisit this issue with a view to three of the historic Reformation confessions: the Belgic Confession,

---

7. See Scott H. Hendrix, *Recultivating the Vineyard: The Reformation Agendas of Christianization* (Louisville: Westminster John Knox Press, 2004).

8. For other examples, see David Bosch, *Transforming Mission: Paradigm Shifts in Theology of Mission* (Maryknoll, N.Y.: Orbis, 1991), 245. Stephen Neill's complete silence about the Reformation speaks volumes in *A History of Christian Missions* (New York: Penguin, 1964). Another book that says nothing about the Reformation is Ruth A. Tucker, *From Jerusalem to Irian Jaya: A Biographical History of Christian Missions* (Grand Rapids: Academie Books, 1983).

the Heidelberg Catechism, and the Canons of Dort. Known as the Three Forms of Unity, these have been widely adopted by Reformed churches around the world. In an earlier book, *For the Cause of the Son of God*, I dealt specifically with the missionary significance of the Belgic Confession at length.[9] Since I did not have the opportunity to explore the Heidelberg Catechism and Canons of Dort in that work, and because these standards remain relatively neglected by missiologists, I intend to demonstrate that all three of these documents have much to offer this field of study.

To say that the Reformation and the confessional documents it produced have little or nothing to say about mission is simply mistaken. Proving that is one goal of this book. The other goal is to help Reformed believers understand their own confessions and how these confessions drive them to care about a world lost in unbelief. Our confessional heritage also leads us to action for those enslaved to sin and unbelief because it is biblical—a faithful summary of the message of God's Word. Contrary to what many missiologists would have us believe, giving more attention to our confessional standards will make us more mission oriented and outward looking, not less.

To be clear, and by way of introduction, this is the definition of mission I will be working with: Mission is the official sending of the church to go and make disciples

---

9. Wes Bredenhof, *For the Cause of the Son of God: The Missionary Significance of the Belgic Confession* (Fellsmere, Fla.: Reformation Media & Press, 2011).

by preaching and witnessing to the good news of Jesus Christ in all nations through the power of the Holy Spirit.[10] I would add that I do not see any biblical justification for a strict distinction between mission and evangelism—in fact, the mission of the church is evangelism. Consequently, my prayer is that this book will serve the glory of God through the advance of the gospel through believers who are ever more eager to share the glad tidings of our great Savior and Lord, Jesus Christ.

I would like to express my gratitude to several people. First, I appreciate the invitation from Rev. Daniel Hyde to write more on this topic. He and Rev. Shane Lems asked me to contribute a chapter regarding the Reformed confessions and mission for a 2011 Reformation Heritage Books volume, *Planting, Watering, Growing: Planting Confessionally Reformed Churches in the 21st Century*. Some of the material from that chapter reappears in this book.

As part of my research, I sent a questionnaire to several Reformed missionaries serving in different parts of the world. Many of their answers to my questions are incorporated in the text. Thanks to Rev. Cornelis Kleyn, Rev. Jim Witteveen, Rev. Glem Melo, Rev. Henk Drost, Rev. Ian Wildeboer, and Rev. Paul Aasman. I know you all are busy men, but I appreciate that you took the time to help.

---

10. Readers who wish to pursue the exegetical development of this definition can refer to chapter 2 of *For the Cause of the Son of God*, by Bredenhof.

I also want to thank Dr. Ted VanRaalte for his advice and assistance with some further research into the Belgic Confession. Last of all, I express thanks to Tim Denbok for his assistance and giving some helpful feedback.

The Belgic Confession

The Belgic Confession is one of a kind: it is the only ecclesiastically adopted confession written by a martyr.[1] It emerges from a dark age of persecution and bears the marks of that age from beginning to end. The 1560s saw many Reformed believers suffer and die for their faith.

Historical Background

Philip II (1527–1598) of Spain ruled over the region known as the Low Countries (Nederlands) during the time the Confession was written. The region was made up of seventeen independent provinces in what is today The Netherlands, Belgium, and part of northern France. Philip was well known for his passionate hatred of any non-Roman Catholic religion. He thought of himself

---

1. At least one other Reformation-era confession, the Guanabara Confession, was written by martyrs. This confession was penned by three Reformed men sentenced to death in Brazil in 1558. It was also the first Protestant confession written in the Americas. However, unlike the Belgic Confession, it was never officially adopted by any church.

as a pillar of the church on a divine mission to eradicate heresy.[2] His being so anxious to prove himself a valiant defender of the faith partly accounts for great bloodshed when the Reformation came to the Low Countries. One author justifiably called the Low Countries "the epicentre of heresy executions in Europe."[3]

The author of the Belgic Confession was Guido (or Guy) de Brès (1522–1567).[4] De Brès was born in 1522, hailing from Mons in the present-day region of southwestern Belgium. His parents were devout Roman Catholics, though it was his mother especially who provided his religious upbringing. In 1547, de Brès was converted to the Reformed faith. Shortly after his conversion, de Brès fled to England, where he received theological training from the Polish Reformer John à Lasco (1499–1560).[5] In 1552, he returned to the Low Countries and became a pastor in Lille. Soon, however, persecutions arose again, and he was

---

2. Robert Collinet, *La Réformation en Belgique au XVIme Siècle* (Brussels: Editions de la Librairie des Eclaireurs Unionistes, 1958), 68.

3. William Monter, "Heresy Executions in Reformation Europe, 1520–1565," in *Tolerance and Intolerance in the European Reformation,* ed. Ole Peter Grell and Bob Scribner (Cambridge: Cambridge University Press, 1996), 57.

4. Not much has been written in English on the biography of de Brès, and certainly nothing at an academic level. However, see Thea B. Van Halsema, *Glorious Heretic: The Story of Guido de Brès* (Grand Rapids: Eerdmans, 1961). In Dutch the latest research is represented by E. M. Braekman, E. A. De Boer, Ruth Pieterman, and Madeleine Gimpel, *Guido de Bres: zijn leven, zijn belijden* (Utrecht: Kok, 2011).

5. E. M. Braekman, *Guy de Brès, I. Sa Vie* (Brussels: Editions de la Librairie des Eclaireurs Unionistes, 1960), 59.

forced to flee to the Protestant regions of Germany and Switzerland. After a short time in Frankfurt, he undertook further studies under Pierre Viret (1511–1571) in Lausanne and then spent some time in Geneva. Eventually the persecutions let up for a time, and de Brès could return to his homeland in 1559. Around the same time he married Catherine Ramon, who was from Tournai, the place where de Brès was serving as pastor. It was during this period, around 1561, that he wrote the Belgic Confession.

Persecutions resumed in late 1561, and de Brès escaped south to France for nearly five years. In 1566 he returned to the Low Countries to become a pastor of the church in Valenciennes. However, soon after returning, the city was rocked by iconoclastic activity that provoked the Spanish authorities to besiege the city during a year that has come to be known as the Wonder Year (*wonderjaar*) in Dutch history. After the siege broke in March 1567, de Brès was captured, and on May 30 he was martyred for his faith. The official charge was celebrating the Lord's Supper contrary to the order of the magistrates. De Brès died a martyr, but the confession he wrote would live on.

As already mentioned, the Belgic Confession was written in the early part of 1561. Its first printing has been pinpointed to May 25, 1561.[6] Very little is known about the exact way in which it was written. It is known that de Brès lived in a discreet spot at the back of a house

---

6. Nicolaas Gootjes, *The Belgic Confession: Its History and Sources* (Grand Rapids: Baker Academic, 2007), 30.

in the neighborhood of St. Brice (or Brixe) and that his study was nearby, close to the walls of the city.[7] It is likely that the Confession was written there, with de Brès doing the greatest part of the work. It is thought that after he wrote it, he shared it with some colleagues who may have given some editorial input toward the final product. Since the two original editions of 1561 have so many printing mistakes, it seems that the Confession was printed rather hastily without much proofreading.[8]

The Confession came to public light later in 1561. However, it appears that by then it had been adopted by the Reformed churches of the Low Countries, or at least some of them. There is evidence of a meeting of ministers in February 1561, and the Confession was probably officially adopted at this meeting. This would also explain the subtitle of the original Confession, which indicates that it was made "in common agreement by the faithful" of the Low Countries. This means that the Belgic Confession was not a personal confession of faith by de Brès that was later adopted by the churches; rather, from the beginning it was an official ecclesiastical confession of faith.[9] This would also explain the use of the first person plural throughout the Confession, beginning with article 1, "We believe...."

After becoming public in fall 1561, the Confession was thrown over the castle wall in Tournai on November 1, and

---

7. Gootjes, *Belgic Confession*, 49.

8. Gootjes, *Belgic Confession*, 32.

9. Gootjes, *Belgic Confession*, 114–15.

it is not known who did this. On October 15, the authorities had discovered a copy of the Confession in the home of Jean du Mortier, a leader in the Reformed church.[10]

In the following year, two more printings appeared. The Confession underwent a revision in 1566 by the Synod of Antwerp, and most of the changes were of a cosmetic nature. The Synod of Dort (1618–1619) also revised the Belgic Confession, established definitive French and Dutch texts, and commissioned a Latin text.[11] Most editions of the Belgic Confession used in Reformed churches today are based on these texts of Dort.

The Belgic Confession is the oldest of the Three Forms of Unity. It is also the one that most bears the marks of John Calvin's (1509–1564) influence, even down to particular expressions or arguments drawn straight from the Genevan Reformer. There were other influences as well, but given that the Belgic has often been regarded as a recasting of the French Confession of 1559 (in the writing of which Calvin had a direct role), it would not be inaccurate to assert that it is essentially Calvin speaking French with a Walloon accent.

As we shall see, the missionary significance of the Confession is intimately tied up with its purpose. It was intended not only to convince the Roman Catholic authorities of the legitimacy of the Reformed churches

---

10. Gootjes, *Belgic Confession*, 17.

11. H. H. Kuyper, *De Post-Acta of Nahandelingen van de Nationale Synode van Dordrecht in 1618 en 1619 gehouden....* (Amsterdam: Hoveker & Wormser, 1899), 107.

and to persuade them to be tolerant, but also, most importantly, to win them to the true gospel of Jesus Christ. Unlike so many today, Guido de Brès and the Reformed churches he served did not regard the Roman Catholic Church as a bearer of the biblical good news, nor did they regard Roman Catholics as brothers and sisters in Christ. Instead, they were regarded as lost and in need of the good news of salvation.

The Belgic Confession is one of the most highly regarded Reformation confessions. It has been adopted by dozens of churches around the world. For example, it is a confession of faith for the Evangelical Reformed Church of Ukraine, the Reformed Churches of Brazil, the First Evangelical Reformed Church of Singapore, and the United Reformed Church in Congo. It has been translated into numerous languages including Portuguese, German, Greek, Russian, Burmese, and Chinese. It has been tested against the Scriptures for hundreds of years and has been found to be a faithful summary of the Word of God.[12] There is little question that it will continue to serve Reformed churches well for coming generations, even as they consider their missionary calling.

---

12. It is true that over the years there have been changes and revisions, some more substantial than others. For example, one well-known case is article 36 regarding what it says about civil government. For some discussion on that, see Bredenhof, *For the Cause of the Son of God*, 192–95. Despite some of these revisions, the overall picture is one of remarkable consistency and faithfulness.

A Missionary Document in the Past

Today, various kinds of documents—tracts and pamphlets, for example—have a missionary purpose. Some books authored by Christians are intended to win the lost to Christ. There are also evangelistic magazines geared toward spreading the gospel message. We might be tempted to think that these sorts of publications are a modern phenomenon. Very few people pause to consider that missionary documents were also written and published during the Reformation. One of those is the Belgic Confession.

The Reformation View of Roman Catholicism

To understand this, we have to come to terms with the way Reformers such as Guido de Brès viewed the Roman Catholic Church and its members. In today's context, many who claim to be Bible-believing Christians have a more positive view of Roman Catholicism, and this has become increasingly evident in contemporary mission studies. Timothy Tennent, for example, writes uncritically of Roman Catholic missionaries spreading the gospel.[13] He refers to them as "brothers and sisters" and depicts the Roman Catholics in Karol Wojtyla's (later, Pope John Paul II) Polish congregation as worshiping Jesus Christ.[14] In recent years, initiatives like Evangelicals and Catholics Together (ECT) and the Manhattan Declaration, which

---

13. Tennent, *Invitation to World Missions*, 254.
14. Tennent, *Invitation to World Missions*, 50, 433.

Tennent signed, have contributed to many Protestants moving away from the Reformation view of Roman Catholicism.[15] According to the consensus view in the Reformation, Roman Catholic Europe was in spiritual darkness. Consistent followers of Roman Catholicism were regarded as unbelievers, the lost in need of the true gospel of Jesus Christ.

Martin Luther (1483–1546), for example, held this view of Roman Catholics. Some of Luther's books were found in the library of Guido de Brès.[16] De Brès had a fondness for Luther and Lutherans—he sought to unite the Reformed churches with the Lutherans in the Low Countries.[17] Luther insisted that much of Europe had been infested with the sixteenth-century equivalent of the Canaanites: "Oh miserable people that we are, to live in these last times so securely and unperturbed among all these Baalites, Bethelites, and Molechites, all of whom appear to be religious and Christian but who have nevertheless swallowed up the whole world and claim that they alone are the Christian church."[18]According to Luther,

---

15. For ECT, see Charles Colson and Richard John Neuhaus, *Evangelicals and Catholics Together: Toward a Common Mission* (Dallas: Word Publishing, 1995), xv–xxxiii. For the Manhattan Declaration, see manhattandeclaration.org.

16. Gootjes, *Belgic Confession*, 62. The original report of the discovery of the library of de Brès is in document 4 in the appendix.

17. Wes Bredenhof, "The Other Confession of Guido de Brès," *Clarion* 60, no. 22 (October 21, 2011): 526–27.

18. Martin Luther, *Luther's Works*, ed. Jaroslav Pelikan (St. Louis: Concordia, 1958–), 36:225–26.

the gospel was not being preached, and where the gospel is not preached, there can be only pagans. Luther called Rome the bride of the devil, the kingdom of antichrist, Satan's whore and synagogue, and other such invective labels.[19] He acknowledged that there were Christians in the Roman Catholic Church before the Reformation and that many essential elements of the Christian faith had been preserved. Yet in the end, it was amply clear that Luther regarded Europe under the pope as a mission field.

However, it was John Calvin who had the greatest influence on de Brès and the Belgic Confession. Calvin's view of Roman Catholics was basically in line with Luther's. In fact, at some points Calvin even goes beyond Luther. For example, he writes in the *Institutes* of how there is no difference between the Romanists and the Turks.[20] When asked if a Christian (a Reformed believer) could marry a Roman Catholic, Calvin replied that the Romanists were outside of Christ, and therefore there could be no marriage in the Lord. Marrying a Roman Catholic was the same thing as marrying a Turk or any other unbeliever.[21] Calvin, too, regarded Roman Catholics as lost in unbelief and therefore as objects for Christian mission.

---

19. Martin Luther, *What Luther Says*, comp. Ewald M. Plass (Saint Louis: Concordia Publishing House, 1959), 1:127; 2:1010; and *Luther's Works*, 41:193–94.

20. John Calvin, *Institutes of the Christian Religion*, ed. John T. McNeill, trans. Ford Lewis Battles (Philadelphia: Westminster Press, 1960), 4.2.10.

21. Hendrix, *Recultivating the Vineyard*, 92.

Guido de Brès shared these opinions. His first book was *The Staff of the Christian Faith* (*Le baston de la foy chrestienne*), published in 1555. It was written partially to win Roman Catholics to the gospel through the use of Scripture and the church fathers. The subtitle of the book identified the Roman church as an enemy of the gospel: *For Arming Ourselves against the Enemies of the Gospel and also for Recognizing the Ancient Pedigree of Our Faith and of the True Church* (pour s'armer contre les ennemis de l'Euangile & aussi pour cognoistre l'anciennete de nostre foy & de la vraye Eglise). Like Luther and Calvin before him, de Brès went on in his book to identify the followers of the pope as pagans and idolaters.[22] There is more evidence of this view in his other writings, but we want to focus on the Belgic Confession.[23]

The Confession continues in the same line. When it was first published, it included a personal appeal to Philip II. This dedicatory epistle was intentionally formulated to incline Philip to read the Confession that followed in the hope that he would be won to the gospel. Today we would expect some restraint, as Philip was a powerful figure and offending him could be very dangerous. However, the Confession is bold in placing Rome outside of the true church of Christ. De Brès outlined how the gospel was lost before the Reformation and denied during it:

---

22. Guy de Brès, *Le baston de la foy chrestienne* (Geneva: Nicolas Barbier & Courtreau, 1558), 4.

23. For more evidence, see Bredenhof, *For the Cause of the Son of God*, 102–10.

From this Confession we trust that you will see that we are wrongly called schismatics, promoters of disunity, rebels and heretics, for we not only uphold and profess the chief heads of the Christian faith, comprehended in the Symbol and Common Creed [the Apostles' Creed], but also the whole teaching, revealed by Jesus Christ, for our life, justification, and salvation, proclaimed by the evangelists and apostles, sealed with the blood of so many martyrs and preserved true and complete by the primitive Church, until at length it was perverted through the ignorance, greed and ambition of the ministers, who have corrupted it with human inventions and traditions contrary to the purity of the gospel, by which our adversaries deny that it is the power of God for the salvation of all believers.[24]

De Brès goes on to intimate that he, and the Reformed churches with him, viewed the broader context as "the world." With due deference he tells Philip that "the world has always hated the light and rebelled against the truth," and instead of thankfully receiving the good news, opposes it.[25]

Following the appeal to Philip, the earliest editions of the Confession included a number of passages on a separate page that provided a biblical basis for confessing the

---

24. This is partly the translation of Alastair Duke, revised to more faithfully reflect the French. Duke's translation can be found in Daniel Hyde, *With Heart and Mouth: An Exposition of the Belgic Confession* (Grandville, Mich.: Reformed Fellowship, 2008), 502.

25. Hyde, *With Heart and Mouth*, 503–4.

faith. These passages also testify to the missionary self-awareness intrinsic to the Belgic Confession. The first passage is Matthew 10:32–33, "Whosoever therefore shall confess me before men, him will I confess also before my Father which is in heaven. But whosoever shall deny me before men, him will I also deny before my Father which is in heaven."

De Brès quotes this passage repeatedly in his other writings. In those places, and here too, there is a particular understanding of the Reformed faith as the only path to salvation; to turn one's back on that faith is to be lost. At the same time, not to confess this same faith is also to be on the broad road leading to destruction.

Next, the Confession quotes Mark 8:38 and the parallel in Luke 9:26. In those passages, our Savior speaks about those who are ashamed of Him "in this adulterous and sinful generation." Jesus says that this does not escape His notice. He will also be ashamed of them. In saying this, Christ implies that confession is a matter of eternal salvation. In quoting these texts, the Belgic Confession maintains that confessing the biblical faith is a matter of one's eternal welfare.

First Peter 3:15 is another favorite passage of de Brès: "But sanctify the Lord God in your hearts: and be ready always to give an answer to every man that asketh you a reason of the hope that is in you with meekness and fear." This text was found on the cover page of most of the first editions of the Belgic Confession and then was repeated on the page with the texts justifying the act of confession.

Peter was clearly writing to Christians living in a pagan world, encouraging them to be always ready to offer a well-considered defense for their faith. When de Brès and the Reformed churches of the Low Countries appropriated these words in the front matter of their Confession, they were indicating their self-awareness of living in a pagan world in need of the gospel.

The last text quoted is 2 Timothy 2:12b, "If we deny [Jesus Christ], he also will deny us." This passage too serves to highlight the seriousness of departing from the true Christian faith. If a person does not hold to the true Christian faith, he cannot claim to be a Christian. This text, like the others, serves to illustrate that the believers in the Reformed churches understood that they were living on a mission field.

Before we consider the articles of the Confession, one more item deserves our attention. When it was first published and for some years following, the Belgic Confession contained an additional title right before the articles: "Truly Christian Confession, Containing the Eternal Salvation of the Soul." It is curious that virtually all modern editions of the Belgic Confession drop these words.[26] The self-understanding implied here does not sit well with modern ecumenical or ecclesiological sensitivities.

---

26. The only exception is the edition found in the Canadian Reformed *Book of Praise: Anglo-Genevan Psalter* (Winnipeg, Man.: Premier Printing, 2014). The *Book of Praise* has slightly altered the words to "True Christian Confession, Containing the Summary of the Doctrine of God and of the Eternal Salvation of Man."

The understanding is that the faith expressed in this confession is the one and only true faith. But do not misunderstand: Our Reformed forefathers were not claiming that there were no other confessions that had expressed the same content in different words or languages. Rather, they were maintaining that the content of this confession, the Reformed faith, is *the* Christian faith.

Articles on the Doctrine of Christ

Now we come to specific articles. Rather than consider the whole body of evidence here, I simply want to draw your attention to some of the articles dealing with the doctrine of Christ and with the church. These will be sufficient to prove that the Confession was designed with a missionary nature and intent.

At the heart of the Confession, we find the articles dealing with the doctrine of Christ. The Reformation doctrine of justification by faith alone is found in article 22. True faith pursues nothing besides Jesus Christ—in Him we find everything we need for our salvation. Therefore, whoever has Jesus Christ has complete salvation: "Therefore, for any to assert that Christ is not sufficient, but that something more is required besides him, would be too gross a blasphemy; for hence it would follow that Christ was but half a Savior."[27] In his other writings,

---

27. James T. Dennison Jr., ed., *Reformed Confessions of the 16th and 17th Centuries in English Translation*, vol. 2, 1552–1566 (Grand Rapids: Reformation Heritage Books, 2008), 424–49. All quotations of the Belgic Confession are from this volume.

de Brès indicts the Roman Catholic Church on this charge of blasphemy. He further outlines how blasphemy is not a feature of the church, but of the world.[28] This gives context to the statement from article 22. To deny justification by faith alone is to blaspheme and to effectively place oneself outside of the church, in the world.

When we get to article 26, we find the same line of thinking. This article speaks of Christ's intercession in heaven, especially as it pertains to the prayers of God's people. Again focusing on Roman Catholicism, the Confession says, "Therefore it was only through distrust [pure lack of trust] that this practice of dishonoring, instead of honoring, the saints was introduced, doing that which they never have done nor required." This is a brilliant way of challenging the Roman Catholic veneration of the saints. The Confession maintains that such veneration is actually dishonor for the saints. But then it goes further and asserts that it is a pure lack of trust (*la seule deffiance*) in Christ. In other words, when Roman Catholics venerate their saints, they are entirely mistrustful toward the Savior Jesus. Consequently, where the saints are honored, there can be no true faith in Christ and consequently no salvation.

Articles on the Doctrine of the Church
In articles 27–32 we find the doctrine of the church. Article 27 makes a reference to the suffering experienced by

---

28. For examples and sources, see Bredenhof, *For the Cause of the Son of God*, 106–7.

those making this confession. It classifies this persecution as being "the rage of the whole world." In article 29, we find some characteristics of the false church. Among other things, the false church is recognized for its persecution of "those who live holily according to the Word of God, and rebuke it for its errors, covetousness, and idolatry." Either the false church is collaborating with the world, or it is to be categorized with the world. What we have seen thus far would favor the latter conclusion.

In article 28, we find confirmation of this with an often quoted and yet often misunderstood statement. It was originally the church fathers Origen and Cyprian who said, "There is no salvation outside of the church."[29] The Reformers did not disagree, and this statement is found not only in Calvin's writings but also in the Belgic Confession. In the Confession, this is the church from which one may—but is not allowed to—withdraw. This is the church with which every believer is obliged to join and unite. This is the church that exists in local believing communities and, in the original context of the Belgic Confession, is to be strictly identified with the Reformed church. The Reformed church was where one would find the marks of the true church mentioned in article 29: the pure preaching of the gospel, the faithful administration of the sacraments, and the proper exercise of church

---

29. See G. Van Rongen, *The Church: Its Unity in Confession and History* (Neerlandia, Alta.: Inheritance Publications, 1998), 79–80; and J. Faber, *Vestigium Ecclesiae: De doop als spoor der kerk (Cyprianus, Optatus, Augustin)* (Goes: Oosterbaan & Le Cointre N.V., 1969), 23.

discipline. To say there is no salvation outside of the church was for Reformed believers to confess that they lived in a context where the church was pitted against the world. Outside of the church is the world of unbelief, of which the false church and sects are a part. Consequently, if one seeks redemption from sin and eternal life, he must be where the marks of the church are found, especially the pure preaching of the gospel.[30]

Continuing with article 28, we find that with regard to the true catholic church, all are duty bound to submit "themselves to the doctrine and discipline thereof; bowing their necks under the yoke of Jesus Christ." Bending one's neck under the yoke of Christ is, of course, an allusion to the words of our Savior in Matthew 11:28–30. This statement in the Confession functions to qualify the unity of the true church of Christ. The Belgic Confession insists that this unity is determined by Jesus' teaching and discipline. People who submit to His teaching and discipline share true unity—and are thus brothers and sisters in Christ. However, the implication is that those who do not so submit are objects of the mission of the church.[31]

---

30. This is not to say that de Brès and other Reformed theologians did not allow for the possibility that individual Roman Catholics, Anabaptists, or others would be saved.

31. For more on the background and meaning of this expression, see W. van't Spijker, "'Den Hals Buygende Onder Het Jock Jesu Christi...' Oorsprong en zin van een uitdrukking in art. 28 en 29 van de Nederlandse Geloofsbelijdenis," in *Bezield Verband: Opstellen aangeboden aan prof. J. Kamphuis*, ed. J. Douma (Kampen: Van den Berg,

Structure and Organization

The original missionary character of the Belgic Confession can also be discerned with respect to its structure and organization, which are dependent on John Calvin's work with the French Confession and his *Institutes of the Christian Religion*.[32] In those writings, Calvin deliberately carried over certain structural elements from medieval scholasticism. These have also been carried over into the Belgic Confession.[33] In particular, we see evidence of what is known as the *locus* method. Doctrine is exposited through a series of well-defined topics; each article deals with a specific topic, and the articles can also be linked together into categories. So, for instance, articles 27–35 contain the doctrine of the church, and each article deals with one or more aspects of that doctrine. The *locus* method can often be seen in the structure of the individual articles as well. A positive statement of faith is given and then supported by biblical evidence. The articles

---

1984), 206–19. For an English summary of van't Spijker, see Van Rongen, *Unity in Confession and History*, 96–100.

32. This is discussed extensively in chapter 4 of Bredenhof, *For the Cause of the Son of God*.

33. On scholasticism in general, see W. J. van Asselt, *Introduction to Reformed Scholasticism* (Grand Rapids: Reformation Heritage Books, 2011). On connections with medieval scholasticism, see David Steinmetz, "The Scholastic Calvin," in *Protestant Scholasticism: Essays in Reassessment*, ed. Carl Trueman and R. Scott Clark (Carlisle, Pa.: Paternoster, 1999), 16–30; and Richard Muller, *The Unaccommodated Calvin: Studies in the Foundation of a Theological Tradition* (New York: Oxford University Press, 2000); chapters 3, 5, and 7 are especially relevant.

sometimes employ logical reasoning. Many of the articles
of the Confession end with the rejection of false teach-
ers. This approach reflects the kind of method used by
medieval scholastic theologians such as Peter Lombard
(1100–1160).[34]

There is also a creedal element discernible in the Belgic Confession's structure. It is not immediately evident
because the first articles deal with the doctrine of God in
general, followed by the doctrine of Scripture. These first
eleven articles form a kind of introduction to the Confession. This kind of introduction, beginning with God
Himself and then moving to His Word, was also charac-
teristic of medieval theology, especially that of the highly
regarded Lombard and his *Sentences*. However, once past
the introductory material, we do find a creedal structure
in the Confession. It proceeds from the Father to the
Son, to the Holy Spirit, and then to the church. Like the
Apostles' Creed, the Confession ends with the doctrine
of the last things.

It is important to realize that Guido de Brès and the
Reformed churches in the Low Countries did have options
for organizing their confession. Some confessions were
written in the form of short statements or theses.[35] Others

---

34. Lombard's most famous work is his *Sentences*. See Peter
Lombard, *The Sentences*, Books 1–4 (Toronto: Institute of Medieval
Studies, 2007–2010).

35. Examples include the Sixty-Seven Articles of Huldrych
Zwingli (1523) and the Ten Theses of Bern (1528), in James T. Dennison Jr., ed., *Reformed Confessions of the 16th and 17th Centuries*, vol.

were written in a chapter-and-article format.[36] There were also catechisms, with their question-and-answer format, but these were seldom written and published to become ecclesiastical confessions of faith.[37] Many Reformation-era catechisms were the product of individual efforts and bore no ecclesiastical authority. Indeed, catechisms were typically prepared as teaching tools and, if widely accepted, only later became established as doctrinal standards to which office bearers were required to subscribe—a rare occurrence.[38] The Reformed churches would have been familiar with these alternatives, and yet they chose the familiar format of a confession organized according to the medieval *locus* method.

There is evidence from *Le baston*, the first book of de Brès, which suggests this structure was adopted intentionally with a view to winning the lost. If you recall, one of the purposes of this book was to win Roman Catholics to the biblical gospel. It was a popular book, and it went through several editions and many printings. It caught the

---

1, *1523–1552* (Grand Rapids: Reformation Heritage Books, 2008), 3–8, 41–42, respectively.

36. For an example, see Luther's Smalcald Articles (1537), in *Concordia: The Lutheran Confessions*, 2nd ed. (Saint Louis: Concordia Publishing House, 2005), 259–85.

37. A classic example of this is the Heidelberg Catechism (1563).

38. Donald Sinnema relates that the Convent of Wesel (1568) expected Dutch Reformed ministers to state their agreement with the Heidelberg Catechism, but formal subscription of the Catechism is not found until 1593. See "The Origin of the Form of Subscription in the Dutch Reformed Tradition," *Calvin Theological Journal* 42, no. 2 (November 2007): 258, 262.

attention of Roman Catholic Church officials too, and it was soon placed on the list of prohibited books.[39] Of particular interest here is the structure of *Le baston*. Initially, the structure followed the *locus* method and presented biblical and patristic citations dealing with eighteen topics. However, in 1559, the Genevan publishing house of Nicolas Barbier and Thomas Courteau published a revised and expanded edition that rearranged the topics and added five more, for a total of twenty-three. Interestingly, the topics in the revised edition more closely follow the Belgic Confession that would appear two years later. Whatever the explanation for that may be, it is clear that de Brès was familiar with the *locus* method for some time before writing the Belgic Confession. He had used this method in *Le baston* to appeal to Roman Catholic readers regarding the ancient biblical and patristic pedigree of the Reformed faith. It is then not surprising that he and the Reformed churches with him would adopt the same method in their confession of faith—with presumably the same purpose.

Other Considerations

We also need to consider some of the more mundane aspects of the Confession. For instance, not many consider the language in which it was originally written to be significant. The Belgic Confession was first written in

---

39. J. M. De Bujanda, *Thésaurus de la littérature interdite au XVIe siècle: Auteurs, ouvrages, editions* (Geneva: Librairie Droz, 1996), 10:97. The Belgic Confession was also on the list of prohibited books.

French. It was soon translated into Dutch, German, and Latin. But we should not take for granted the original tongue. After all, in this era, many Protestant confessions were still written in Latin. The Belgic Confession was written in Walloon French to reach the francophone masses in the Low Countries. A confession in Latin would have signaled an international audience of pastors and scholars; however, a confession in the vernacular clearly signaled a popular audience.

The original published format was also geared to mass consumption. Today the Belgic Confession usually appears as part of a church hymnal or psalter. However, it was originally published by itself as a booklet in a small format known as an octavo.[40] Publishers in areas such as the Low Countries appreciated the small size because it meant the project was finished and out on the market quickly. This was important where the Roman Catholic authorities were seeking to suppress Protestant publishing.[41] Moreover, this format was cheap to produce and consequently available on the market at low cost. The original octavo format of the Belgic Confession also made it discreetly portable—it could easily fit into shirt and coat pockets.

---

40. Also abbreviated 8°, an octavo was produced by taking a full printer's sheet (about 25 x 30 inches) and folding it three times to result in a booklet with the dimensions (when trimmed) of 7 x 10 ¾ inches.

41. Andrew Pettegree, *Reformation and the Culture of Persuasion* (Cambridge: Cambridge University Press, 2005), 149.

Often commentators define the sole purpose of the Belgic Confession in a defensive manner. In their view, the Belgic Confession was written only to defend the Reformed churches against the charge that they were holding to novel doctrine. In particular, the Reformed believers wanted to distance themselves from the Anabaptists, especially the more radical ones. They were trying to win toleration from the authorities who viewed them as a threat to civil order and decency. It is true that the Confession did have this as *part* of its original purpose. However, as has been demonstrated, we need to see that it had a missionary purpose as well. The Confession not only stood defensively, but it also actively witnessed to the world of unbelief.

A Missionary Document in the Present

The Belgic Confession witnessed to the world in sixteenth-century Europe, but the question is whether it can still function that way today. My research shows that it can and does. Reformed missionaries in every corner of the world still use the Belgic Confession in their labors for the gospel.

Rev. Paul Aasman, for example, is a Canadian Reformed missionary who was called to work in downtown Hamilton, Ontario. He has been doing that work since 2006. Many of the people with whom he has contact are on the lower end of the socioeconomic scale and have suffered with addictions and mental illness. Aasman explains that "without a doubt, the Belgic Confession is the most useful confessional tool in my work.... It is apologetic in nature, persuasive in intent, eloquent and comprehensive for the main points of Christian doctrine. This makes it ideally suited to introducing inquirers to the faith." Before making a public profession of faith in the missionary congregation he serves, prospective members are expected to follow a seven-month course of study based on the Belgic Confession.

In the western reaches of Ukraine is the small city of Rivne. Until 2014, Rev. Henk Drost lived and worked there as a missionary of the Reformed Churches in the Netherlands—Liberated (*Gereformeerde Kerken—Vrijgemaakt*). He also speaks highly of the Belgic Confession as a tool on the mission field. Drost notes the original missionary function of the Confession and maintains that it still has that function today. This confession tells outsiders what we believe. Additionally, it can also be effectively used to train and disciple young believers for witnessing. The Belgic Confession has been translated into Russian and Ukrainian, the two languages most widely spoken in Ukraine. Like the original format in 1561, the Confession is available in Ukraine as a small booklet that can be cheaply and easily distributed.

Heading to the Asia-Pacific region, a number of Reformed missionaries are working in Papua New Guinea. Among them is Rev. Ian Wildeboer, a Canadian missionary under the oversight of the Free Reformed Churches of Australia. Rev. Wildeboer reports that the Belgic Confession is a newcomer to this country, only having been recently translated into the English Creole language known as Tok Pisin. It is being used in Papua New Guinea as a guide for upper-level instruction for adults in missionary congregations. Says Wildeboer, "Although maybe not as easy to teach as the Q/A format of the Heidelberg Catechism, we find that the Belgic Confession fleshes out teachings (inspiration and authority of Scripture, true church/false church) that nicely complement the Catechism. We have enjoyed some lively discussions among both newer and older members on the teaching of the Belgic Confession."

A Confession for a Missional Church

Not only does the Confession have a function as a missionary document, but it also inspires and directs Reformed churches to be missional or outward looking.[42] Here I simply want to draw your attention to a few of the Confession's statements in its section on the doctrine of the church.

Article 27 expresses the Reformed doctrine regarding the catholicity of the church. Catholicity has several facets. Temporal catholicity refers to the church's existence from the beginning of the world to the end. Cultural or social catholicity refers to the church being found among every tribe, tongue, and nation. Closely connected with cultural catholicity is geographical catholicity. The church comes to expression all over the world. The two last facets

---

42. See Bredenhof, *For the Cause of the Son of God*, especially chapter 5.

of catholicity are mentioned in the concluding paragraph of article 27: "Furthermore, this holy Church is not confined, bound, or limited to a certain place or to certain persons, but is spread and dispersed over the whole world; and yet is joined and united with heart and will, by the power of faith, in one and the same spirit."

This is an important statement, for it acknowledges that there is broadness in God's plan of salvation. The church is made up of diverse peoples living all over the globe. In His good pleasure, God has gathered these people into His church. From this we can discern the truth that it is God's will to gather people from all nations into His church. He has done it in the past and is doing it in the present, and there is every indication from Scripture that He desires to continue doing it in the future. Catholicity reveals God's intention that His church be global. Being a global church necessarily implies missionary activity.

Of the articles on the doctrine of the church, article 29 is probably the most well known among Reformed church members. It describes the marks of the true and false church. First among the marks of a true church is the pure preaching of the gospel. We might think that this too implies missionary activity. Certainly the gospel must be preached in established churches, but it should be a given that the gospel would also be preached to the lost at home and overseas.

However, a difficulty arises with some modern editions of the Belgic Confession. Compare, for instance, the version adopted by several Reformed churches with the edition having a more accurate translation:

> Modern edition:"If the pure doctrine of the gospel is preached therein...."

> More accurate translation: "It practices the pure preaching of the gospel...."

The key difference is the word "therein," and at least two problems arise with its inclusion in article 29. The first is that the word did not appear in the original Belgic Confession of 1561. It also never appears in any subsequent French, Dutch, or Latin editions. "Therein" seems to appear out of thin air in the English edition adopted by the Reformed Dutch Church in the United States of America (now known as the Reformed Church of America) in 1792.[43] It has remained with most English versions ever since.

The second issue is far more important: Is it biblical to restrict this mark to what goes on in the church? Here is a place where the original 1561 Belgic Confession can help us. Matthew 28:18–20, the Great Commission, is one of the proof texts for this statement in the original confession.[44] In this passage, Jesus sends His disciples

43. *The Constitution of the Reformed Dutch Church in the United States of America* (New York: William Durell, 1793), 28.

44. Guy de Brès, *Confession de foy, faicte d'un commun accord par les fideles qui conversent ès pays bas* (Rouen: Abel Clemence, 1561), 24. From the beginning, the Belgic Confession included proof texts to indicate the biblical basis of its teachings. For some recent discussion of the history and role of these proof texts, see Nicolaas Gootjes,

out to preach, teach, and disciple "all nations." Clearly the original intent of the Belgic Confession was to include the missionary calling of the church under the first mark.[45] A church that does not faithfully proclaim the gospel both inside and outside its membership has a credibility problem when it comes to being a true church. The word "therein," then, should be excised from all English editions of article 29. The way in which the Belgic Confession shapes missional churches is certainly enhanced if we move closer to the original text.

Last, there is an important statement in article 30 regarding the government of the church. Through the divinely ordained offices of the churches, it is God's intent that "the true religion may be preserved and the true doctrine everywhere propagated." Here again, we encounter a problem with the text of the Belgic Confession. Not all editions agree on the exact wording here. The text quoted above is what most editions follow, and it is essentially a translation of a highly respected Latin edition commissioned by the Synod of Dort (1618–1619). However, the Synod of Dort adopted only authoritative French and Dutch editions that have a different wording that is reflected in the edition adopted by the Canadian Reformed Churches: "By these means they preserve the true religion; they see to it that the true doctrine takes

Teaching and Preaching the Word: Studies in Dogmatics and Homiletics (Winnipeg, Man.: Premier Publishing, 2010), 298–300.
45. See Calvin Van Reken, "The Mission of a Local Church," *Calvin Theological Journal* 32, no. 2 (November 1997): 359.

its course." Notice that there is no mention of the true
doctrine being propagated everywhere. Instead, "the true
doctrine takes its course." How do we resolve this?

Once again it is helpful to look back at the very first
editions of the Confession. From the proof texts used,
we can get a sense of what de Brès and the Reformed
churches intended by this statement. The text used with
this statement is Galatians 2:8, "For he that wrought
effectually in Peter to the apostleship of the circumci-
sion, the same was mighty in me toward the Gentiles."[46]
Peter was entrusted with ministry to the Jews and Paul
to the Gentiles. Both had their own calling in their own
place. Both office bearers were called to propagate the
true doctrine, and between them, this true doctrine was
being propagated everywhere. From this it appears that
the Latin commissioned by the Synod of Dort is a faithful
rendering of what the Confession originally intended to
say. The true doctrine taking its course is the same thing
as the true doctrine being propagated everywhere.

So the Confession clearly ties the missionary calling of
the church to the offices of the church. It is the responsibility of the office bearers of the church to ensure that the true
doctrine of the gospel is proclaimed everywhere it must
be proclaimed—all over the world. Therefore, mission
must be an agenda item for Reformed consistories. They
must send out, support, and oversee the work of mission
in our own country and elsewhere. The Belgic Confession

---

46. De Brès, *Confession de foy*, 27.

assigns this responsibility to the church's leaders in article 30. In this and more ways, the Belgic Confession drives Reformed churches to be outward looking and enthusiastic about mission.

The Heidelberg
Catechism

Benjamin Breckinridge Warfield (1851–1921), "the Lion of Princeton," was not only a subscriber to but also a vocal proponent of the Westminster Shorter Catechism. His enthusiasm for the Shorter Catechism led him to be critical of other Reformed catechisms. So, for instance, Warfield critiqued the Heidelberg Catechism for being man centered rather than God centered. Since it allegedly takes its starting point in man's comfort rather than in God's glory, the Heidelberg Catechism falls short, he believed. He went so far as to say that the Catechism's voice is one of "a sort of spiritual utilitarianism, a divine euthumia."[1] How can a catechism that starts with man be truly Reformed?

Warfield's critique has not been persuasive.[2] Most readers and confessors of the Catechism recognize that

---

1. B. B. Warfield, "The First Question of the Westminster Shorter Catechism," *Princeton Theological Review* 6, no. 4 (October 1908): 565. "Euthumia" refers to a pleasant state of mind.

2. See, for example, Fred H. Klooster's critique of Warfield in *Our Only Comfort: A Comprehensive Commentary on the Heidelberg*

a concern for God's glory pervades it. Moreover, they are immediately impressed with its personal and experiential nature. This catechism drives biblical truth home not only to the mind but also to the heart and will. Its theme, structure, and content are scriptural, and its appeal is holistic. For good reason pastors often read from the Catechism at hospital beds and graveside services. While the first question and answer with its classic opening lines—"What is your only comfort in life and death?"—is a frequent choice, many others offer comfort as well.[3]

Historical Background

How did this amazing catechism come about? Like the Belgic Confession, the Heidelberg Catechism has a unique quality. It is a Reformed catechism out of a German-speaking region—a region typically associated with Lutheranism. Somehow the Reformed faith as confessed by men like Calvin and Farel carved out a niche in a German territory known as the Palatinate. Behind all this was an influential ruler named Frederick III (1515–1576).

Frederick, the son of Duke Johann II (1515–1576), had been born and raised as a Roman Catholic in the Duchy of Simmern. By 1548 he was a Protestant, having come to Lutheran convictions through his marriage

---

Catechism (Grand Rapids: Faith Alive Christian Resources, 2001), 1:42–47.

3. On the Heidelberg Catechism, see *A Faith Worth Teaching: The Heidelberg Catechism's Enduring Heritage*, ed. Sebastian Heck and Jon Payne (Grand Rapids: Reformation Heritage Books, 2013).

in 1537 to Maria of Brandenburg. In 1559, Frederick became elector of the Palatinate. His predecessor, Otto Henry (1502–1559), had exhibited tolerance for people with Reformed convictions, but it was really under Frederick that Reformed theology was not merely tolerated but promoted and even required.

When Frederick took the title of Elector Palatine, he was still a Lutheran. However, a debate erupted in the church at Heidelberg regarding the Lord's Supper. Tilemann Hesshus (1527–1588) was the general superintendent of the church, and he held to the strict Lutheran view of the sacrament. Opposing him was deacon Wilhelm Klebitz (1533–1568), a staunch defender of the Reformed position. The details of this debate are not important for our purposes here, but the debate forced Frederick to make a careful theological study of the matters at hand. The more he studied, the more he began moving toward the Reformed stance. A debate was held in Heidelberg in 1560 on the Lord's Supper that definitively pushed Frederick to the Reformed confession.[4]

Frederick's shift to Reformed convictions meant changes not only in the churches of the Palatinate but

---

4. Wim Verboom, "The Completion of the Heidelberg Catechism," in *The Church's Book of Comfort*, ed. Willem Van't Spijker (Grand Rapids: Reformation Heritage Books, 2009), 36. For more on the Lord's Supper controversy in Heidelberg see Charles D. Gunnoe Jr., "The Reformation of the Palatinate and the Origins of the Heidelberg Catechism, 1500–1562," in *An Introduction to the Heidelberg Catechism: Sources, History, and Theology*, ed. Lyle D. Bierma (Grand Rapids: Baker Academic, 2005), 37–42.

also in the theological faculty at the university in Heidelberg. The elector became eager to attract Reformed pastors and theological professors. This brought two notable young men to Heidelberg. Twenty-three-year-old Caspar Olevianus (1536–1587) arrived in 1560, and twenty-seven-year-old Zacharias Ursinus (1534–1583) came a year later.

Olevianus was born in Trier.[5] As a teenager he studied in France and became a Protestant there. After completing his university studies in law, Olevianus went to Switzerland to study with Reformers such as Calvin. He returned to Trier in 1559 to teach logic and philosophy, but eventually his Protestant convictions put him in conflict with the Roman Catholic majority in the city. This brought him to Heidelberg in 1560. While he started off as an instructor of pastors, eventually he became a pastor.

Ursinus hailed from Breslau, a city in present-day Poland.[6] He was born into a Lutheran family—the Reformation had been introduced in the 1520s. In 1550, Ursinus began studies under Philip Melanchthon (1497–1560) at the university in Wittenberg. After completing his studies in 1557, the young man toured Europe and along the way made the acquaintance of other Reformers.

---

5. This biographical information has been summarized from "The Purpose and Authorship of the Heidelberg Catechism," in *An Introduction to the Heidelberg Catechism: Sources, History, and Theology*, by Lyle D. Bierma (Grand Rapids: Baker Academic, 2005), 57–59.

6. This biographical information has been summarized from Bierma, "Purpose and Authorship of the Heidelberg Catechism," 67–71.

In 1558, at age twenty-four, he took a position teaching classical languages and Christian doctrine at the St. Elizabeth School in his hometown of Breslau. However, like his future colleague Olevianus, Ursinus soon ran into difficulties back home, though not with the Roman Catholics but with strict Lutherans who would not tolerate his view of the Lord's Supper. This led him to spend a year in Zurich studying under Peter Martyr Vermigli (1499– 1562). In 1561, having heard high praise for Ursinus, Frederick III invited him to come to teach in Heidelberg. Ursinus accepted, and before long he was teaching theology to future pastors.

Ursinus and Olevianus have often been identified as the main authors of the Catechism—indeed, the editions used by most Reformed churches today still identify them as such. The impression has sometimes also been given that it was a joint effort, with Ursinus contributing theological acumen and Olevianus pastoral warmth. This impression has been called into question in the last century. The latest research by Lyle Bierma argues that the Catechism was the work of a committee. Ursinus did most of the work—he probably had primary responsibility for the final draft, organized the elements of the Catechism, and provided proper connections between each question and answer.[7] And yet the evidence also suggests that "Olevianus played a more significant role in the

---

7. Bierma, "Purpose and Authorship of the Heidelberg Catechism," 74.

composition of the [Heidelberg Catechism] than most recent scholarship has recognized."[8]

The purpose of the Catechism has been far less controversial. Elector Frederick III composed a preface to the Heidelberg Catechism that clearly indicates why he commissioned it.[9] It was written to regulate the religious instruction of the youth of the Palatinate. Pastors and schoolmasters were often creating their own catechisms or using a variety of other existing catechisms. Consequently, there was no consistency or guarantee of theological faithfulness. Frederick presented them with this request in the preface:

> We ask that you diligently and faithfully represent and explain the Catechism according to its true meaning to the youth in our schools and churches, and also from the pulpit to common people you teach. We ask that you act and live in accordance with it. Have the assured hope that if our youth are early on instructed earnestly in the Word of God, it will please the Almighty also to grant reformation of public and private morals, and temporal and eternal welfare.[10]

---

8. Bierma, "Purpose and Authorship of the Heidelberg Catechism," 66–67.

9. This preface can be found in English in *We Believe: The Creeds and Confessions of the Canadian Reformed Churches*, ed. Wes Bredenhof (Hamilton, Ont.: Providence Press, 2010), 151–53; George W. Richards, *The Heidelberg Catechism: Historical and Doctrinal Studies* (Philadelphia: Publication and Sunday School Board of the Reformed Church in the United States, 1913), 183–99.

10. Bredenhof, *We Believe*, 153.

While the focus was on the youth of the churches, this catechism was also intended to instruct older people. We might think, then, that the Catechism was designed with an inward-looking orientation. However, we should also note Frederick's concern for reformation within his realm that included the eternal welfare of his subjects.

It was not long before the Heidelberg Catechism was recognized as a first-class work. In the same year it was published it was translated into Latin and Dutch. An English translation appeared in 1572. Over the years, the Catechism has been translated into numerous other tongues and adopted by hundreds of Reformed churches around the world. Its pastoral character carries a universal appeal, and, as we shall see, this is one of the reasons so many Reformed missionaries love and use it.

The Heidelberg Catechism as a Missionary Document

At first glance, the Heidelberg Catechism seems to have a place only in the established church of Christ. Throughout its questions and answers, it uses the first-person singular pronouns *I*, *me*, and *my*, so that it seems that the catechumen is already a Christian. For example, the student answers regarding the holy catholic church that "I am and forever shall remain a living member of the same." It seems difficult to discern a missionary thrust to the Catechism.

However, if we go back to the original historical setting, we soon discover that there is more here than meets the eye. By the time the Catechism was written, the Palatinate was officially Protestant. Moreover, Elector Frederick III was obviously leaning toward the Reformed confession. We could say that the region under his rule was Reformed, yet there is an important caveat to bear in mind. In 1555, the Peace of Augsburg established the principle known in Latin as *cuius regio, eius religio,* which literally means "of whom the region, his the religion." In other words, regions of the Holy Roman Empire would follow the religious convictions of their rulers. This is how it would be on paper. In reality, however, many of the people on the ground would have had other convictions or maybe even none at all.

We know this to be the case from Frederick III. In the original preface to the Heidelberg Catechism, Frederick noted how many of the youth in his realm had "often grown up without the fear of God and the knowledge of his Word."[11] It is important to note that the Protestant Reformation had only begun to take root in the Palatinate in 1545.[12] By the 1560s, there was still much gospel ignorance in Frederick's realm, and the Heidelberg Catechism was envisioned partly as a means of addressing this problem. As we saw above, he viewed it as his responsibility to promote not only the temporal welfare of his subjects but also their eternal welfare. He was particularly concerned for the youth: "It is essential

---

11. Bredenhof, *We Believe*, 152.

12. Fred H. Klooster, "Missions—The Heidelberg Catechism and Calvin," *Calvin Theological Journal* 7, no. 2 (November 1972): 195.

that our youth be trained in early life, and above all, in the pure and consistent doctrine of the holy Gospel and that they be well-versed in the proper and true knowledge of God."[13]

How do we reconcile that evangelistic or missionary purpose of Frederick III with the language and approach of his catechism? The answer is that no reconciliation is required because there is no real conflict. The Catechism can be taught in such a way that it is evident that these are the answers a true Christian gives. These are the answers that everyone must give who would live forever. An unbelieving catechumen can be just as much evangelized with these answers as the believing catechumen can be instructed and discipled. After all, does not the same twofold process happen today in every established Reformed church where the Catechism is taught and preached? This twofold process was intrinsic to the original purpose of not only the Heidelberg Catechism but many other Reformation-era catechisms as well.[14]

As an instrument of the Reformation in the Palatinate, the Heidelberg Catechism can certainly be regarded historically as a missionary document. The Reformation was not merely about getting people to change religious or ecclesiastical affiliations. It was about bringing people to the true gospel of Jesus Christ so that they would find abiding life in Him. Frederick III felt the urgent need to

---

13. Bredenhof, *We Believe*, 152.
14. Pettegree, *Reformation and the Culture of Persuasion*, 190.

hasten this gospel ministry, and this was an important reason he commissioned the Catechism. There can be little question that Frederick's reformational program "was so urgent that home missionary motives were present as well."[15]

Of the Three Forms of Unity, the Heidelberg Catechism is the confession that has most often been used by Reformed missionaries past and present. Surprisingly, one of the first languages into which the Catechism was translated was Hebrew by a Reformer who had been converted from a Jewish background, Immanuel Tremellius (1510–1580). The purpose of the translation was purely missionary: to win Jews for Christ.[16] Today the Catechism has been freshly translated into modern Hebrew and is being used as an outreach tool among Jews in Israel.[17]

Two examples from history show how the Catechism has been used in mission work in Brazil. Frans Schalkwijk has written a fascinating study of the Reformed church in Brazil from 1630 to 1654, when the Dutch had colonial settlements in this part of the world. Not only had they established Reformed churches with these settlements, but they also made mission efforts among both native inhabitants and the Portuguese. Schalkwijk notes that the Heidelberg Catechism was second in importance after

---

15. Klooster, "Missions," 197.

16. Klooster, "Missions," 207.

17. David Kranendonk, "Hamas, HaGefen, and Heidelberg," *Open Doors: The Mission Magazine of the Free Reformed Churches* 1, no. 1: 13.

the Bible for evangelistic work among the Portuguese.[18] Johannes Apricius was a Reformed minister doing missionary work among the Tupí peoples indigenous to Brazil. He was making efforts to translate the Heidelberg Catechism into the Tupí language. Before he could fully succeed, however, the Dutch were being expelled from Brazil by the Portuguese.[19]

Today the Heidelberg Catechism continues to be used by Reformed missionaries around the world with great profit. Rev. Glimar Melo is a former Pentecostal missionary who now does Reformed missionary work in Cagayan de Oro on the island of Mindanao in the Philippines. He comments, "I found the Heidelberg Catechism most helpful because it contains all the basic truths that all Christians need to learn, is easy to teach and very pastoral. It is highly effective in building faith and encouraging a life of thankful obedience for believers." Also in the Philippines, Rev. Adrian Helleman served as a Christian Reformed missionary for several years in Quezon City, on the island of Luzon. In an article for *The Banner* about the use of the Heidelberg Catechism in missionary work, Helleman explains:

> People in the Philippines receive the Catechism enthusiastically. One day I handed a copy (written in the local language) to an inquirer. I saw him again a few days later. His first comment to me was, "I

---

18. F. L. Schalkwijk, *The Reformed Church in Dutch Brazil (1630–1654)* (Zoetermeer: Uitgeverij Boekencentrum, 1998), 155–57.

19. Schalkwijk, *Reformed Church in Dutch Brazil*, 181, 227.

stayed up the whole night. I read it from cover to cover." Talk about enthusiasm! Not long after that some men who had been studying the Catechism with me only a few weeks asked how they could become members of my church. Other Christian Reformed missionaries in the Philippines have had similar experiences.[20]

Helleman is unapologetic about teaching the controversial question and answer 80 regarding the accursed idolatry of the Roman Catholic Mass.[21] He concludes by pointing out that if the Catechism can be useful in the Philippines for evangelistic purposes, there is no reason why it could not be similarly useful in North America, especially in evangelizing Roman Catholics.

---

20. Adrian A. Helleman, "The Heidelberg Catechism and Missions," *The Banner* 119, no. 32 (September 10, 1984): 6–7.

21. Contrast this with the current position of the Christian Reformed Church (CRC) on question and answer 80. In its edition, the CRC explains: "In response to a mandate from Synod 1998, the Christian Reformed Church's Interchurch Relations Committee conducted a study of Q&A 80 and the Roman Catholic Mass. Based on this study, Synod 2004 declared that 'Q&A 80 can no longer be held in its current form as part of our confession.' Synod 2006 directed that Q&A 80 remain in the CRC's text of the Heidelberg Catechism but that the last three paragraphs be placed in brackets to indicate that they do not accurately reflect the official teaching and practice of today's Roman Catholic Church and are no longer confessionally binding on members of the CRC." See the 2011 version of the Heidelberg Catechism, Christian Reformed Church, http://www.crcna.org/welcome/beliefs /confessions/heidelberg-catechism. The CRC believes that the Roman Catholic Church has changed its teaching on the Mass. However, the Roman Catholic Church maintains that it has not changed its doctrines.

Other missionaries have expressed appreciation for the structure and format of the Heidelberg Catechism. Rev. Cornelis Kleyn, a Canadian Reformed missionary in Papua New Guinea, notes that he constantly uses the Catechism in his work. His colleague, Ian Wildeboer, adds that the sin–salvation–service structure of the Catechism provides missionaries with a memorable, biblical, and effective teaching tool. Moreover, the question-and-answer format inherently allows for a more interactive learning scenario.

Rev. Jim Witteveen is a Canadian Reformed missionary working in the city of Prince George, British Columbia. He started this work in 2008, and through his efforts and under the blessing of God, a small Reformed congregation is developing. Many of the people with whom Witteveen comes into contact have a Baptist background. He reports that the section of the Catechism that deals with the sacraments has been exceptionally helpful, especially for clearing up misconceptions regarding what Reformed churches actually believe about the sacraments.

In Ukraine, Rev. Henk Drost has also found the Catechism helpful. He sees it as important for training young missionary congregations in the basics of the faith and in thinking apologetically about their faith and how they share it. It is also used to disciple new members and bring them into church membership. However, the Catechism can also have a direct role in the early stages of evangelism:

> It is my experience that the Heidelberg Catechism is a great tool for introducing people to the Reformed

faith and the Reformed church. It all starts in the catechism with Jesus, who is our comfort. But already in Lord's Day 2, it teaches about our sin and misery. That is an essential point to speak about with people who want to be members of a Reformed church. We have to know if they understand what grace is and how to live in it. The Catechism is a touchstone for whether you can admit people to the church or not.

Drost has also served established Reformed congregations in the Netherlands. There he also regularly used the Catechism's summary of biblical teaching to stimulate God's people to take seriously their evangelistic calling in this dark world. As we shall see in the next section, the Catechism certainly leads God's people to be outward looking. Even if they are not called to serve officially as missionaries, all of God's people are called to have missionary hearts, and the Catechism soundly drives that home.

A Catechism Pointing Us Outward

Leading up to the 450th birthday of the Heidelberg Catechism in 2013, some Reformed young people in Hamilton, Ontario, created a video in which they asked people on the street the first question of the Catechism: "What is your only comfort in life and death?"[22] They approached people with the Catechism's first question. One man answers, "Doing good for your family." A young man answers, "Sitting on my couch and watching TV."

22. See the video here: https://www.youtube.com/watch?v=dKpc _206Wls.

A boy answers, "Having my family to support me." Still another young man says, "Just living life and living in the moment." While a number of people were approached, only one man answered, "Christ." What this video tells us is that there are many people who have an answer to this first question of the Heidelberg Catechism. But most of their answers are shallow, and most of the people who responded did not really think about death. Instead, they were concerned only about comfort in life. They would rather not talk about death. This sort of video is helpful because it reminds us that there are many people out there who are lost, and when death comes they will *not* have comfort. Their deaths will be sad in every respect because their lives were wasted on shallow comfort.

Question and answer 1 is well known as a faithful summary of biblical teaching. It also encapsulates the theme and tone of the entire Catechism. Comfort in life and death comes from belonging to Christ from the beginning of one's earthly life to its end—and beyond. Comfort in life and death is found in the fact that the sins of believers have all been paid for with the blood of Christ. Comfort in life and death includes the preservation of a heavenly Father. The lives of believers are under His providential care so that even the most seemingly insignificant things do not happen by chance. Comfort in life and death comes from the assurance of the Holy Spirit in the hearts of believers. He tells them that they are God's children, and He makes them want to live as God's children, loving and serving Him. In short, the only comfort in life and death comes down to the gospel, which really carries believers along through each day and gives strength in the face of death. The gospel gives confidence that there is far more beyond death.

This gospel of comfort in life and death is what the lost need. What the Catechism outlines in its first question and answer is what sinners on their way to hell need in order to be saved. They need to say this, to make this their confession of faith too. Why? Because it is *biblical*.

As we survey the Heidelberg Catechism, there are places where we explicitly see our need to bring this gospel message to the lost. We need to lay this out because, unfortunately, there are still those who argue that the Heidelberg Catechism produces churches that are inward looking and insular. They say that the Catechism makes us dead to the calling we have from the Bible to be witnesses for Christ. I argue that if that happens and we are poor letters of Christ, the fault must be only our own, not the Catechism's. If believers read the Catechism carefully and really believe what it says, the inevitable result will be outward-looking communities of believers who care about the lost and are compelled to bring them the gospel by whatever means possible.

Outward-Looking Prophets

Question 32: But why art thou called a Christian?

Answer: Because by faith I am a member of Christ, and thus a partaker of his anointing; in order that I also may confess his name, may present myself a

living sacrifice of thankfulness to him, and may with
a free conscience fight against sin and the devil in this
life, and hereafter, in eternity reign with him over
all creatures.

I will begin by drawing attention to the first element of
what we call the office of every believer. As a member
of Christ, every believer is called to be a prophet who
confesses His name. This is part of what it means to be
a Christian.

The title "Christ" refers to the anointing of our Lord
Jesus by the Holy Spirit to a threefold office of prophet,
priest, and king. He is the prophet par excellence, whose
role is to teach believers through His Word. His prophetic calling involves communication with the words of
the Bible. No one today on earth watches Jesus to see how
He lives. He is in heaven at God's right hand, so we cannot see or watch Him. The only way Christians can be
the recipients of Christ's prophetic communication is by
paying attention to the words given in Scripture.

By faith and the Holy Spirit who works faith, believers are united to Christ. They are grafted into Him like
branches would be grafted onto a tree. Thus they share in
His anointing and therefore also in His threefold office.
Believers share in the prophetic side of this office as well.
Part of the biblical basis for that can be found in 1 Peter
2:9, where the apostle Peter says that his readers are
a royal priesthood. They are kings and priests. He says
that they are a holy nation. Then he adds that they are "a
peculiar people; that [they] should shew forth the praises

of him who hath called [them] out of darkness into his
marvellous light." Belonging to God brings with it a consequence: prophetically declaring His praises. According
to Peter, believers are to be speaking of the wonderful
grace of God in Christ that has brought them from darkness to light. They should do that with everyone they can,
both inside and outside the church—with fellow believers, but also with the lost in the world.

Acts 11 also makes this point. Persecution led the
church to be scattered all over the Roman Empire. As
Christians moved into new environs, they were speaking a
message, according to Acts 11:19. Some people might say,
"We don't have to say anything about the gospel. Our life-
style will say it all." Others might quote the words of that
old song, "They will know we are Christians by our love."
Still others quote the words often wrongly attributed to
Francis of Assisi (1181/82–1226), "Preach the gospel at
all times—if necessary, use words."[23] But we ought to look
carefully again at Acts 11 to see what the church did there.
Believers *spoke* of the wonderful grace of God in Christ.
They lived out of union with Christ, and that meant also
actively being prophets confessing His name. They told
people *with words* the good news about the Lord Jesus.
The result: "a great number of people believed and turned
to the Lord."

---

23. Even though this saying is often attributed to Francis, there
is no evidence that he ever said or wrote it. No one appears to know
where the saying really originates.

Reformed believers simply cannot escape from what is confessed in question and answer 32. In his commentary on the Catechism, Ursinus writes that the prophetic office consists first in rightly knowing God and His will. That knowledge obviously comes from Scripture. But then he goes on to say that it also includes "that every one in his place and degree profess the same, being correctly understood, faithfully, boldly, and constantly, that God may thereby be celebrated, and his truth revealed in its living force and power. 'Whosoever shall confess me before men, him will I also confess before my Father which is in heaven' [Matt. 10:32]."[24]

God's truth must be revealed—the truth found in the words of Scripture. Believers are called to be prophets confessing the name of Christ. As He is confessed with words before men, so also He will confess believers, laying claim to them with words before the Father. So "prophets confessing" means that believers are going to be speaking with words about their only comfort in life and death in the gospel. A silent prophet is unimaginable. No one could conceive of a prophet in the biblical sense as a mime with no words to speak. Christian prophets are called to communicate with words, just like their Savior

---

24. Zacharias Ursinus, *The Commentary of Dr. Zacharias Ursinus on the Heidelberg Catechism*, trans. G. W. Williard (repr., Phillipsburg, N.J.: P&R, 1985), 179. Ursinus goes on to speak of an outward-looking direction in the office of priest as well. It includes, "1. To teach others; that is, to show and communicate to them the knowledge of the true God.... 4. Confession of the gospel. 'Ministering the gospel of God, that the offering up of the Gentiles might be acceptable' (Rom. 15:16)."

communicated, still communicates, and will communicate. If believers look in faith to Christ and if they are united to Him, then what is true of Him must also be true of them.

It has to be that way for all Christians. Being a prophet is not just a hobby or interest for some Christians. It is the calling of all Christians, young and old. The opportunity may not always be there to carry out this calling. Yet there should always be readiness and expectancy on the part of believers. They should be praying for the Lord to bring opportunities and looking for them. Sometimes Christians have a level of discomfort or uncertainty about how to pursue this in a concrete way. If that is the case, they should find a way to address this, like a course such as Two Ways to Live, which teaches Christians how to share the gospel naturally and winsomely.[25]

Before moving on, I should clarify. Besides the Christian's calling to prophetically speak about his only comfort in life and death, he also has a calling to live a Christian life. This calling also has an outward-looking goal. Question and answer 86 speaks about our sanctification. Why must we do good works? Part of the answer is so that "by our godly walk of life we may win our neighbors for Christ." When believers live out of union with Christ, they walk in His ways, and the hope is that even when they are voicing no words about Christ, people will see

---

25. For more information on Two Ways to Live, see http://www
.matthiasmedia.com.au/2wtl/whatis2wtl.html.

that Christians are different because of Christ. We want people to become curious about what makes us different so that they will ask us, and then we will have the opportunity to speak about our hope in the gospel. However, no one should conclude from this that having a godly walk of life is the only calling of a Christian with respect to the lost. The Bible speaks differently, and so does the Heidelberg Catechism. Reformed believers are to have a godly walk of life, *and* they are to confess the name of Christ with their words whenever and to whomever they can. The two are not opposed to one another, and one is not a substitute for the other.

An Outward-Looking People

Question 54: What dost thou believe concerning the Holy Catholic Church?

Answer: That out of the whole human race, from the beginning to the end of the world, the Son of God, by his Spirit and Word, gathers, defends, and preserves for himself unto everlasting life, a chosen communion in the unity of the true faith; and that I am, and forever shall remain, a living member of the same.

In this question and answer, we want to focus on the first thing the Son of God does. When Christians confess with the Apostles' Creed that they believe a holy catholic church, they confess that the Son of God *gathers* this church. This is something He has done from the beginning of the world, and He will continue doing it until the end. Moreover, this is something that involves the whole human race. He gathers people into His church from every culture on the face of the earth.

Andrew Walls, a professor of mission, gives a good illustration of this.[26] He suggests we imagine an intergalactic time traveler who comes to earth from time to time to study Christianity. He first comes in the year 37 to Jerusalem and sees that almost all the Christians are Jews who are eager to share the good news about the Messiah with as many people as they can. The next time the researcher comes to earth it is 325, and he visits the Council of Nicea. There are hardly any Jews at all in attendance; in fact, the members of the group are diverse, from all kinds of cultures. They are in an intense debate about how Jesus is related to God the Father and the type of language that should be used to speak about such things. In the 600s the traveler comes back, this time to Scotland. He encounters Celtic monks calling people to faith and repentance. They use the formula and language decided on at the Council of Nicea. On his next trip, the intergalactic traveler arrives in London, England, in the 1840s. A large meeting of Christians is proposing to send missionaries to Africa. He is surprised to see that most of these people have their own copy of the Bible. On his last journey, the traveler ends up in Lagos, Nigeria, in 1980. It is a Sunday, and he sees crowds of Africans joyfully on their way to church to hear preaching about Jesus Christ.

---

26. Andrew Walls, "The Gospel as Prisoner and Liberator of Culture," in *The Missionary Movement in Christian History: Studies in the Transmission of Faith* (Maryknoll, N.Y.: Orbis, 1996), 3–7.

Indeed, Christ has been gathering His church out of the whole human race throughout history. That process started long before AD 37—it started with the creation of Adam and Eve, and Christ is busy continuing to draw people to Himself today. The Heidelberg Catechism speaks here of the glorious work of Christ in growing His church. How does He do this?

It certainly does not happen automatically. Christ uses means, or instruments, to gather His church. The Heidelberg Catechism follows Scripture here and tells us what those means are: the Holy Spirit and the Word of God. Yet this needs to be unpacked more. For instance, how does Christ bring His Word to the lost so that they are gathered into His church?

The answer is that He works through His body, the church, to bring His Word to the lost. The church of Christ is His messenger, entrusted with His Word, which speaks of the gospel, the only comfort in life and death. There are two ways in which this happens.

One is through the official ministry of the church. The church sends out men called to be missionaries with the gospel of Christ. They are sent out in an official capacity to preach the gospel, to bring in lost souls, to disciple them, and to establish more churches. These missionaries might be working in or near their home country, perhaps in a difficult urban setting or with an immigrant community or in foreign countries. The gospel can also be administered to the lost in established churches in public worship on Sundays. Believers are encouraged to bring their unbelieving friends to church to be exposed to the means of grace, especially to hear the preaching—to be convicted by the law and of their sin so that they turn to the gospel of Christ with repentance and faith. As Michael Horton points out, public worship should also be the place where unbelievers face "a disrupting encounter with a holy and gracious God…in the regular celebration of the Supper."[27] Together with the preaching of the word, the sacraments do not merely prepare us for mission; they are actually part of a missionary event, "as visitors are able to hear and see the gospel…and the communion that it generates."[28] So the ministry of the church through its office bearers, whether they are missionaries or regular ministers, is one way in which Christ gathers His church.

But Christ also gathers His church through the witnessing of the ordinary members. As believers care about the lost God has put on their path, they pray for opportunities to speak of their hope and for courage to seize those opportunities. They do seize them and then speak about the comfort that is found in belonging to Jesus Christ. As God's people have done that faithfully and prayerfully over the years, Christ has worked through them to gather His church.

As the church brings the word of Christ to unbelievers, she can also look for and depend on the work of the Spirit of Christ. The Holy Spirit works miracles. He is the one

---

27. Michael Horton, *The Christian Faith: A Systematic Theology for Pilgrims on the Way* (Grand Rapids: Zondervan, 2011), 901.

28. Horton, *Christian Faith*, 902.

who softens hard hearts and opens closed eyes. He works through Christians to bring people to faith. Thus, when believers have this gospel treasure in Christ, the comfort of belonging to Him, the Holy Spirit not only compels them to love their lost neighbors, but He also gives them the strength to share the gospel. The church cannot be outward looking by her own strength and resources. She needs the Spirit of Christ to equip her and strengthen her for this calling.

Being Outward Looking Prayerfully

> *Question 123*: What is the second petition?

> Answer: Thy kingdom come. That is: So govern us by thy Word and Spirit that we may submit ourselves unto thee always more and more; preserve and increase thy Church; destroy the works of the devil, every power that exalteth itself against thee, and all wicked devices formed against thy holy Word, until the full coming of thy kingdom, wherein thou shalt be all in all.

In this question about the Lord's Prayer, the Lord Jesus teaches believers to pray for the coming of the kingdom. The Catechism expands on what that means. Part of what it means is that they are praying for God to increase His church.

What does "increase" mean here? Martin Luther produced one of the first Bibles in German, working from the original languages of Hebrew and Greek. Luther's complete German translation was first published in 1534 and is widely recognized as one of the great forces shaping the development of the German language. The Heidelberg Catechism was first written in German too. In question 123, the Catechism originally used the same word Luther used in his translation of Genesis 1:28, "Be fruitful and increase in number," or "Be fruitful and multiply."[29] The Catechism is teaching that believers should pray for God to increase the numbers in His church.

That this is the correct understanding of the Catechism is confirmed by comparison with the Larger Catechism of Zacharias Ursinus. He has a parallel question and answer regarding the second petition of the Lord's Prayer:

> *Question 246*: What are we asking for with these words?
>
> Answer: That God sanctify believers more and more by his Spirit, add to their number, and restrain those who fight against him, until, when all obstacles have been removed, it becomes plain that all things are subject to his will.[30]

Clearly Ursinus understood the second petition to involve a missionary or outward-looking orientation.[31] With the Catechism, Reformed confessors understand that we are called to pray for church growth.

---

29. The Heidelberg Catechism: "erhalt und *mehre* deine kirchen." Luther's translation of Genesis 9:7, "Seid fruchtbaar und *mehret* euch und reget euch auf Erden, daß euer viel darauf warden."

30. See the translation of the Larger Catechism in Bierma, *Introduction to the Heidelberg Catechism*, 208.

31. See Ursinus, *Commentary on the Heidelberg Catechism*, 633, 636.

However, they must pray for that from the heart with an attitude that desires increased numbers in the church. Do Reformed churches want to see more people coming to them seeking the only comfort in life and death? Here is where fear and mixed-up priorities sometimes can be crippling. Believers may fear that if they pray for more numbers in their local church, God will hear and actually answer them. Priorities then come into play, because if there are more people, there are going to be more problems with seating, room may be at a premium, and the church is probably going to have to spend more money. Therefore, some might think that common sense dictates that it is foolish to pray for increased numbers in the church.

Yet this is what Reformed churches confess in the Heidelberg Catechism. God teaches believers through Scripture to pray for the church to grow. Is God's Word foolish, and are we irresponsible to follow it? Would God have believers deny or ignore this part of His Word because of financial considerations? It should be obvious that this would not be pleasing to God; instead it would be rank worldliness and unbelief. Reformed churches must take their confession seriously. These Reformed confessions bind us together in the unity of faith. What we have in the Heidelberg Catechism is what we say we believe. If this is what we say we believe, we must live by it.

Living according to what we believe begins with a healthy and positive attitude about growth in numbers. We should want our churches to grow, not so much from what we call the circulation of the saints, or transfer growth. We should want our churches to grow from God adding people plucked out of the world, turned around from sin and brought to faith in Christ. Our desire should be to see new believers added to our numbers through conversions. Yes, if God answers our prayer for increase in the way we desire, there may be challenges. Yet He will provide the means. We must trust that He will lead us forward. He will bless our desire to be an outward-looking church with a heart of compassion for the lost. We have to trust our faithful God.

With that attitude of faith, believers can and should all pray in the spirit of the second petition. We can pray fervently for God to grow our churches. We can pray that He add to our numbers, not for the sake of numbers but for the glory of His name and because we genuinely care about our unbelieving friends and neighbors.

The Heidelberg Catechism is now over 450 years old. Some critics say that 450 years ago the church did not care about the lost and really did not have an outward-looking perspective the way Christians do today.[32] It should be readily evident that this is simply not true. This Reformation catechism points us outward as churches, telling us about how we will care for and engage the lost

---

32. For example, Samuel Volbeda, who taught mission at Calvin Seminary from 1926 to 1952, argued that the Three Forms of Unity (including the Catechism) are "practically devoid of missionary material. They are mum on the matter of missions." Quoted in Kevin Allen Schutte, "The Missional Church and New Church Development in the CRCNA" (MA thesis, Calvin Theological Seminary, March 2003), 5.

as we live in union with Jesus our Savior. It faithfully summarizes the teaching of Scripture about the calling of the church to be a light in the darkness. Believers have a great comfort in life and death in Christ. That great comfort is certainly worth sharing.

3

The Canons of Dort

For a few years in their early history, the Reformed churches in the Netherlands had two forms of unity, not three. The Belgic Confession and the Heidelberg Catechism made up the doctrinal foundation that bonded the Dutch Reformed churches together. For about two decades, these confessions functioned fairly well as tools to guard the deposit of biblical truth handed down from the apostles. Things began to change when a man named Jacobus Arminius (1560–1609) came on the scene.[1]

Before Arminius, there had been doctrinal dissenters in the Reformed churches. More particularly, there had been those who questioned the formulation of the

---

1. For biographies of Arminius, see Carl Bangs, *Arminius: A Study in the Dutch Reformation* (Nashville: Abingdon Press, 1971); and Keith D. Stranglin and Thomas H. McCall, *Jacob Arminius: Theologian of Grace* (Oxford: Oxford University Press, 2012). For his theology, see William den Boer, *God's Twofold Love: The Theology of Jacob Arminius (1559–1609)* (Göttingen: Vandenhoeck & Ruprecht, 2010).

doctrine of election in article 16 of the Belgic Confession.[2] However, it was Arminius who became the most influential figure in the push to reconfigure the doctrines of grace in the late sixteenth century.

Historical Background

Who was this Arminius? He was born Jakob Harmenzoon in 1560 in the town of Oudewater in the province of Utrecht. He had a tumultuous upbringing, losing both father and mother at a young age. Various theologians took an interest in the orphan while he was still a youngster, and it was under the influence of one of them that Arminius was able to take up the study of theology at the University of Leiden in 1576. He finished his studies there in 1582 and then moved to Geneva to study with Calvin's successor, Theodore Beza. By 1588, he was back in the Netherlands, called to be a pastor of the Reformed Church in Amsterdam. While there had already been hints of troubles earlier in Geneva, Arminius's preaching in Amsterdam was really what put him in the center of theological controversy.[3]

---

2. Louis Praamsma discusses these "precursors of Arminianism" in some detail. See "The Background of the Arminian Controversy (1586–1618)," in Crisis in the Reformed Churches: Essays in Commemoration of the Great Synod of Dort, 1618–1619, ed. Peter Y. De Jong (1968; repr., Wyoming, Mich.: Reformed Fellowship, 2008), 41–44.

3. While he was in Geneva as a student, Arminius was already at odds with Theodore Beza over both the content and method of predestinarian theology. Despite their differing views, however, they maintained a friendly relationship. See Richard A. Muller, God,

He preached a provocative series of sermons on Paul's letter to the Romans. He reportedly made remarks that his complacent listeners would have been better off staying in the Roman fold, since then at least they would be motivated to do good works. Arminius claimed that man would have died even apart from the fall into sin because only God is immortal. Echoing the sentiments of many of his modern-day followers, Arminius maintained that Romans 7 was speaking about Paul in his unregenerate state. When he exposited Romans 9 and 11, he placed the emphasis on human free will.[4] There were more such controversial statements that led his ministerial colleagues especially to be suspicious of his orthodoxy. However, when pushed, Arminius would always affirm his willingness to maintain the Reformed confessions.

The plague intervened to take Arminius away from his pastorate in Amsterdam in 1602. Two theology professors at Leiden, Franciscus Junius (1545–1602) and Lucas Trelcatius (1542–1602), were struck down by the deadly disease. Arminius, recognized as a man of learning and someone who might moderate "the fanaticism of some," was appointed to take the place of Junius. This happened even though both Junius himself on his deathbed as well as the only remaining theological professor, Franciscus Gomarus

---

(1563–1641), disapproved.[5] Nevertheless, Arminius continued to assert that he held Reformed convictions and was permitted to take up his teaching post. Though he taught for only seven years, through his work at Leiden Arminius was able to develop a cadre of enthusiastic disciples.

About a year after his death in 1610, these followers issued a statement in five points. This was called the Remonstrance (which means "complaint"), and from this point on, the followers of Arminus would be known as Remonstrants. Today we have five points of Calvinism because there were first five points of the Arminians. In these five points, the Remonstrants reformulated the Reformed doctrine of election and other doctrines that follow from it.

Controversy continued in the Reformed churches through the second decade of the seventeenth century. Eventually an international gathering, or synod, was convened in the Dutch city of Dordrecht (Dort) to deal decisively with the issues being raised by the Remonstrants.[6] Most of the delegates were from the Dutch

---

5. H. J. Meijerink, "The Origins of the Canons of Dort," in *The Bride's Treasure: Introduction to the Canons of Dort*, by J. Faber, H. J. Meijerink, C. Trimp, G. Zomer (Launceston, Tasmania: Publication Organisation of the Free Reformed Churches of Australia, 1979), 15–16.

6. Unfortunately, not much has been written on the history of the Synod of Dort. For general history, two more recent volumes are Aza Goudriaan and Fred van Lieburg, eds., *Revisiting the Synod of Dort (1618–19)* (Leiden: Brill, 2011); and W. van't Spijker, C. C. de Bruin, H. Florijn, A. Moerkerken, and H. Natzijl, *De Synode van Dordrecht in 1618 en 1619* (Houten: Den Hartog, 1987). For treatments of

Reformed church, but there were also several foreign delegations. Among them were British, German, and Swiss delegates. The French were also invited but were prevented from coming by their king.

This was a long synod—it lasted from November 1618 to May 1619. Many decisions were made, but it was especially the Arminian issue that put this synod in the history books and resulted in the writing of the Canons of Dort. Some of the Remonstrants were ordered to present their views to the synod. The Remonstrants were resistant and sabotaged the synod's efforts to reach a clear understanding of their views. They refused to recognize the authority of the synod and were generally uncooperative. On January 1, the States-General decided that if the Remonstrants would not cooperate with the synod, their views would be judged solely on the basis of written evidence, with no opportunity for oral presentations or defenses.[7] Eventually on January 14, 1619, with fire in his eyes, the synod chairman, Johannes Bogerman (1576–1637), dismissed the Remonstrants, and the synod proceeded without them.

---

two particular issues at the Synod see W. Robert Godfrey, "Tensions within International Calvinism: The Debate on the Atonement at the Synod of Dort, 1618–19" (PhD diss., Stanford University, 1974); Donald Sinnema, "The Issue of Reprobation at the Synod of Dort (1618–1619) in Light of the History of This Doctrine" (PhD diss., University of St. Michael's College, Toronto, 1985).

7. Donald Sinnema, "The Drafting of the Canons of Dordt: A Preliminary Survey of Early Drafts and Related Documents," in *Revisiting the Synod of Dort (1618–19)*, ed. Aza Goudriaan and Fred van Lieburg (Leiden: Brill, 2011), 314.

There were still tense moments after the departure of the Arminians. It was not easy for all these Reformed theologians to reach a consensus on how best to respond to these false teachings. All agreed that the Remonstrants were wrong and that their teachings needed to be corrected, but there were differences of opinion on such finer points as infra- and supralapsarianism, and these presented a serious challenge to formulating the Canons. Delegations presented different formulations for discussion, and sometimes the discussions were heated. At one point, Gomarus even challenged the Bremen delegate, Matthias Martinius (1572–1630), to a duel, illustrating how high emotions ran. Yet, by God's grace, in the end the delegates were able to find one another on the basis of the Word of God. The result was the Canons of Dort.

The document was originally written in Dutch, French, and Latin. Each of the five points of the Remonstrants was addressed with a positive statement of doctrine in a chapter, or "head"—however, the two points concerning total inability and irresistible grace were combined into one since they were regarded as closely connected. Each chapter ends with a "Rejection of Errors" section. Remonstrant writings are directly quoted and then addressed with biblical teaching. The original editions of the Canons included a preface and a conclusion. The conclusion is usually included with modern editions, but the preface is more difficult to find.[8]

---

8. It can be found in an appendix in *We Believe*, ed. Bredenhof, 156–59.

The Canons of Dort are a remarkable blend of theological precision and experiential warmth. This confession was produced during the era of early scholastic orthodoxy, and its writers were all trained in scholastic methods. Some aspects of scholasticism are more evident in the Canons than in the Belgic Confession or Heidelberg Catechism. This is understandable since the issues at hand were so theologically intricate that they required the best theological tools available—which, in this era, meant scholastic methods. Yet this document was produced primarily for the churches, and not for the academy.[9] The Canons of Dort reflect a serious concern for Christian piety among lay believers and demonstrate how the doctrines of grace have a profound impact on the church in her calling in this world.

Today the five points of Calvinism are virtually synonymous with the Canons of Dort. Because of a resurgence of interest in the doctrines of grace, there has also been increased attention given to the Canons of Dort. Today the Canons are available in at least two dozen languages around the world. Wherever the Canons travel, the doctrines of grace triumph. Just as holy synods of old, the Synod of Dort, in its own words, "removed the seed of error and of discord, preserved the Church in the unity

---

9. See W. Robert Godfrey, "Popular and Catholic: The *Modus Docendi* of the Canons of Dordt," in *Revisiting the Synod of Dort (1618–19)*, ed. Aza Goudriann and Fred van Lieburg (Leiden: Brill, 2011), 243–60.

of the pure religion, and passed on the genuine religion
unblemished to posterity."[10]

A Missionary Document?

Of the Three Forms of Unity, the Canons of Dort would
be the most unlikely to be considered a missionary document in any meaningful sense. As we have seen, the Belgic
Confession was composed as a witness to the surround-
ing context of unbelief and wrong belief. The Heidelberg
Catechism was written primarily as a teaching tool, but
the original intent—to instruct those who didn't have a
full understanding of the gospel—means that it has a missionary orientation. The Canons of Dort, though, were
written as a polemical confession to clarify certain points
of doctrine from the Belgic Confession and the Heidelberg Catechism and guard against the false teachings of
the Remonstrants. Is it possible to discern anything of a
missionary orientation in this confession?

In 1972 *Calvin Theological Journal* dedicated an issue
to the Three Forms of Unity and mission. Anthony
Hoekema wrote the article dealing with the Canons of
Dort. He concluded "that the Canons of Dort certainly
do express the missionary focus of the Bible."[11] He found
that the Canons were strong on missionary theology,
but weaker with respect to missionary responsibility.[12]

---

10. Bredenhof, *We Believe*, 157.

11. Anthony A. Hoekema, "The Missionary Focus of the Canons
of Dort," *Calvin Theological Journal* 7, no. 2 (November 1972): 219.

12. Hoekema, "Missionary Focus of the Canons of Dort," 220.

However, Hoekema did not discuss the Canons of Dort as a missionary document; evidently they did not stand out to him as being such a document. It seems that no one has ever described the Canons as such.

This is understandable. The Canons were written for the distinct purpose of protecting the Reformed churches from Arminian error. They were composed to ward off false doctrine by providing clear and concise summaries of biblical teaching on the doctrines of grace. Nothing in the Canons themselves or in any associated documents suggests that the fathers at Dort wrote this confession with the intent to win the lost.

However, is it possible that though the Canons were not originally intended to win the lost, they may still have functioned in that capacity? Here we have to consider carefully the seriousness of the Arminian errors. If we survey the language of the synod in the "Rejection of Errors" (RE) section that follows each head of doctrine, we get a clear picture of how Arminianism should be evaluated. The following are some of the terms used: "error" (1.RE 1); "offensive error" (1.RE 3); "gross error" (1.RE 6); "they bring back out of hell the Pelagian error" (2.RE 3); "pernicious poison of Pelagianism" (2.RE 6); "innovation" (3/4. RE 3); "entirely Pelagian and contrary to the whole Scripture" (3/4.RE 7); and "outright Pelagianism" (5.RE 2). Pelagianism was condemned as a heresy by the Council of Carthage in 417–418. The church then declared that those holding to Pelagian views were anathema—in other words, eternally condemned and outside of salvation.

This continued to be the church's view after the Reformation. The post-Reformation church did not take a more tolerant view of Pelagianism than the pre-Reformation church—if anything, quite the opposite. The harsh and direct words of the Synod of Dort have to be understood against this background. Dort was saying that the Arminians, insofar as they might hold to Pelagian positions, are lost. Strictly speaking, consistent Arminians are not saved because they are not holding to the biblical gospel of free grace in Christ alone. This might be an unpopular position to maintain today, but this is what the Canons of Dort assert in as many words.

The Canons of Dort were not written to persuade the Arminians of their errors. They did have this effect, but only on a small scale. Following the Synod of Dort, some forty pastors with Remonstrant convictions were persuaded back to the Reformed doctrines of grace. They subscribed the Canons of Dort and were restored to their churches.[13] However, these were exceptions. For the most part, the Synod of Dort recognized it was dealing with men who were deeply entrenched in their positions. The majority of the Remonstrants had invested much in their Arminianism and would not easily be convinced, even with the sound biblical arguments the synod produced. No, the Canons were composed to protect the Reformed churches from these errors. They were written especially

13. H. Kaajan, *De Groote Synode van Dordrecht in 1618–1619* (Amsterdam: N. V. De Standaard, 1918), 183.

to persuade those who might be tempted to swing in the Arminian direction. This is evident from the conclusion of the Synod of Dort:

> Therefore, this Synod of Dort adjures, in the name of the Lord, all who piously call upon our Saviour Jesus Christ not to judge the faith of the Reformed churches from the slander gathered from here and there. Neither are they to judge from personal statements of some ancient or modern teachers, often quoted in bad faith, or taken out of context and explained contrary to their meaning. But one ought to judge the public confessions of these churches themselves and from the present explanation of the orthodox doctrine, confirmed by the unanimous consent of the members of the entire Synod, one and all.

The synod went on to warn the Arminian slanderers of the judgment of God that awaited them for bearing false witness, upsetting weak believers, and bringing suspicion on the Reformed churches. However, there was really no hint of a conscious effort to persuade and win the Arminians. The time for that was long past. This was the time for judgment and admonition.

Nevertheless, the Canons have been instrumental in bringing some to true faith. In chapter 1, we learned how Europe had become a mission field before the Reformation. Some decades after the writing of the Canons of Dort, deformation set in again. Unbelief was widespread. The light of the gospel was not entirely extinguished, but things were grim. By the early years of the 1800s, most Reformed churches in the Netherlands were Reformed merely in name, as were their leaders. The worst sorts of rationalism and liberalism had come to dominate. The gospel was nearly eclipsed, along with our biblical Reformed heritage. Men would become pastors without ever having heard of John Calvin, much less having read him. Preachers would often subscribe the Three Forms of Unity without ever having studied them.

One such pastor was Hendrik de Cock (1801–1842). His seminary training at the University of Groningen was largely unbelieving and rationalistic. He graduated in 1823 and became a typical Reformed pastor of the time—which is to say, a preacher of morality. He too subscribed the Reformed confessions, but his signature meant little since he had never really studied them.[14] If he was not entirely lost spiritually, he was certainly mired in serious error. One writer compares him to Saul, Augustine, and Luther before their conversions.[15] P. Y. De Jong (1915–2005) described him as not having experienced a

---

14. By this time the Form for Subscription had become ambiguous anyway. After 1816, ministers promised that "we in good faith accept and heartily believe the doctrine which, conformable to God's Holy Word, is contained in the adopted Forms of Unity of the Nederlansche Hervormde Kerk." The word "conformable" (*overeenkomstig*) left a major loophole for doctrinal dissent, and it was often exploited. For the full text of the Form for Subscription signed by de Cock and other pastors in this era see R. C. Janssen, *By This Our Subscription: Confessional Subscription in the Dutch Reformed Tradition Since 1816* (Kampen: Theologische Universiteit, 2009), 47.

15. G. Keizer, *De afscheiding van 1834: haar aanleiding, naar authentieke brieven en bescheiden beschreven* (Kampen: J. H. Kok, 1934), 141.

spiritual awakening.[16] This process of awakening began, however, when he took up a pastorate in the small village of Ulrum in the northern province of Groningen.

De Cock started meeting with Klaas Pieters Kuipenga, an adult member of the congregation who had not made public profession of faith. Surprisingly, De Cock learned more from his student than his student learned from him. Kuipenga's clear understanding of the Reformed doctrine of depravity is clear from his oft-quoted words: "If I had to add only one sigh to my salvation, I would be lost forever." That made an impression on de Cock. The next step in the process involved the discovery of an abridgement of Calvin's *Institutes*, which led de Cock further. A booklet by C. Baron Van Zuylen entitled *The Reformed Doctrine* awakened the pastor even more to the errors he and so many others held. The last stage in the process of de Cock's awakening involved the Canons of Dort. A member of his congregation gave him a copy. After eight years of serving as a Reformed pastor, de Cock finally read and eagerly studied the Canons of Dort, and this confession brought him to embrace fully the biblical gospel of grace. De Cock was so enthused with his rediscovery that he republished the Canons of Dort at his own expense in 1833. This was de Cock's first publication, and it included his preface. From this point forward, the Canons would not be forgotten again in the Reformed churches in the

---

16. P. Y. De Jong, "The Dawn of a New Day," in Hendrik Bouma, *Secession, Doleantie, and Union: 1834–1892* (Neerlandia, Alta.: Inheritance Publications, 1995), 238.

Netherlands. Partly because of the Canons of Dort, one man was led to the saving truths of the gospel, and a whole new reformational movement was ignited: the Secession (*Afscheiding*) of 1834.

Today Reformed missionaries carry the Canons of Dort with them around the world. My research shows that the Canons are not typically regarded as a missionary document. The enthusiasm of most Reformed missionaries is reserved for the older creeds, the Belgic Confession and the Heidelberg Catechism. The Canons are widely considered only as an advanced instructional tool for new believers.

For example, missionary Paul Aasman comments that the Canons are the meat to be served after the milk. He uses this confession for the instruction of believers after they are admitted as members of the church. However, he mentions that the doctrines of the Canons are always in the background of his preaching and teaching. Should objections arise to the doctrines of grace, the Canons of Dort can be quite useful as a teaching tool. In the Philippines, Glem Melo concurs. He states, "The Canons of Dort are useful in instilling God-centeredness in the minds and hearts of new believers." But such instruction comes later in the process of catechesis.

However, we should not forget those who claim to be Christians and yet hold to the Arminian doctrine of salvation, either ignorantly or self-consciously. If they are holding to these doctrines consistently, there is at least a question mark behind their eternal welfare. Thankfully, most Arminians do not hold to their theology consistently.[17] Moreover, there are degrees of Arminianism, and degrees to which people hold to these views. Yet for the salvation of some and the consistent giving of all the glory to God by all, Reformed missionaries will continue to teach the Canons of Dort to Arminians too. For example, missionary Jim Witteveen has found the Canons to be indispensable for his labors. He remarks:

> I have constantly been impressed with the pastoral nature of this confession; it's more than just a doctrinal treatise on "the five points of Calvinism," and this has proven to be very helpful in teaching people who have come to the church from a fundamentalist Baptist background…. Interestingly, I've found that new Christians have far less problem with the Canons of Dort than those who come to us from different church backgrounds!

17. See James Montgomery Boice and Philip Graham Ryken, *The Doctrines of Grace: Rediscovering the Evangelical Gospel* (Wheaton, Ill.: Crossway, 2002), 36. Boice and Ryken recount the famous exchange between the Calvinist Charles Simeon and the Arminian John Wesley, in which Simeon concludes that the gulf is not so great between them. They conclude: "Wesley was hardly a Calvinist, but perhaps it may be said that he was a Calvinist at heart. He instinctively recognized the truth of a principle that he had not yet worked into his theology with consistency, namely, that sinners contribute nothing to their own salvation—it is God's work from beginning to end. He knew that in order for the gospel to be a gospel of grace it must be all of grace." Similarly, B. B. Warfield noted that all true Christians are Calvinists on their knees. See "What Is Calvinism?," in *Selected Shorter Writings of Benjamin B. Warfield*, ed. John E. Meeter (repr., Phillipsburg, N.J.: Presbyterian and Reformed, 1970), 1:390.

Therefore, a confession written in response to the Arminians continues to be useful for persuading those who hold to these views on modern-day mission fields.

Perhaps the Canons of Dort are most relevant as a confession that provides some theological foundations for the church's missionary task. This is Henk Drost's view. He maintains that the abiding value of the Canons of Dort is really that they give a Reformed vision for evangelism and mission. This applies especially to established churches, but it can also apply to fledgling missionary congregations as well. The Canons of Dort provide us with valuable direction on how and why we should be a missionary church. We'll explore this point more in the final section of this chapter.

The Canons of Dort and Missionary Theology

There are several key ways in which the Canons of Dort guide our missiology. One has to do with the question of what happens to those who have never heard the gospel. Billions in the history of the world have lived and died without hearing about Jesus Christ. What do we say about their eternal destination?

Missiologists offer several different answers. Some are inclusivists.[18] Inclusivism teaches that through general revelation, non-Christians have access to the saving grace

---

18. John Hick is a well-known representative. See "A Pluralist View," in Dennis Okholm and Timothy R. Phillips, eds., *More Than One Way: Four Views on Salvation in a Pluralistic World* (Grand Rapids: Zondervan, 1995), 29–59.

of God in Christ, even if they have never heard of Jesus. Others are pluralists.[19] Pluralism holds that all the world's religions provide access to salvation. Believers in other religions simply must be sincere in what they believe. Still others hold to some form of postmodern view.[20] A typical postmodern approach to this question acknowledges that all religions are different with little to no common ground between them. These religions should engage respectfully in dialogue, but always in recognition of the fact that they are exclusive of one another. Those taking this approach answer the question of what happens to unbelievers by proposing that we should envision "multiple goals, multiple salvations, and multiple deities." Surveying this view but not endorsing it, Tennent writes, "The classic pluralist metaphor of many paths up one mountain has been replaced in [this] model with many paths up many different mountains."[21]

Along with the other Reformed confessions, the Canons of Dort repudiate these ways of thinking, upholding an exclusive way of salvation: through faith in Jesus Christ alone. Our confession echoes the teaching of Scripture in John 14:6: the only way to the Father is through Christ.

As a consequence, one cannot expect that a religion of works will be of any saving value. The Canons of Dort

---

19. Clark H. Pinnock holds this position. See "An Inclusivist View," in *More Than One Way*, 95–123.

20. For example, S. Mark Heim, *Salvations: Truth and Difference in Religions* (Maryknoll, N.Y.: Orbis, 1995).

21. Tennent, *Invitation to World Missions*, 205.

maintain that man is totally incapable of any saving good. Furthermore, they assert, "Without the regenerating grace of the Holy Spirit, they are neither able nor willing to return to God, reform the depravity of their nature, nor to dispose themselves to reformation" (3/4.3). While unregenerate man possesses the *sensus divinitatis*, or light of nature, no one uses it correctly. Rather than having any saving worth, it serves to make a person inexcusable before the just Judge of heaven and earth (CD 3/4.4). Article 5 of chapter 3/4 likewise insists that the law is insufficient to bring anyone to peace with God. The line of argument reaches its apex in article 6: "What, therefore, neither the light of nature, nor the law could do, that God performs by the operation of his Holy Spirit through the word or ministry of reconciliation: which is the glad tidings concerning the Messiah, by means whereof it hath pleased God to save such as believe, as well under the Old as under the New Testament."

From that line of argument in chapter 3/4 of the Canons, we glean the principle that mission work has a necessary place in the scheme of God's kingdom. If men were not commissioned and sent out with the gospel of salvation, the kingdom would not advance. We cannot expect people to be saved from God's just wrath apart from the missionary ministry of the church. Both Scripture and our confessions teach that salvation is found only in Jesus Christ, so His good news must be universally and indiscriminately proclaimed. This point is reinforced earlier in the Canons: "Moreover the promise of the gospel is, that whosoever believeth in Christ crucified shall not perish, but have everlasting life. This promise, together with the command to repent and believe, ought to be declared and published to all nations, and to all persons promiscuously and without distinction, to whom God out of His good pleasure sends the gospel" (2.5).

What the Canons teach us is the sound biblical doctrine that mission is not optional for the church—rather, it is an essential part of God's work in this world. If our local churches are not eagerly involved in mission at home and abroad, we cannot blame the Canons of Dort—or any of our confessions. Instead, if we neglect mission, our confessions witness against us.

When we think about the Canons of Dort, our thoughts usually go to the doctrines of grace they exposit and especially the Reformed doctrine of election. We believe that God works in time to gather those whom He, in His good pleasure, has elected in Christ from before the foundation of the world. Sadly, this biblical doctrine has often been maligned in the name of mission.

Many authors in both the past and present have claimed that belief in the Reformed doctrine of election results in a lack of zeal for missionary work. Often they refer to a story about William Carey (1761–1834), a Particular Baptist missionary to India who is known as "the father of modern missions." When Carey presented his plan to evangelize the world, a Calvinist colleague named John Ryland (1723–1792) reportedly rebuked him by saying, "Young man, sit down; when God pleases to convert the heathen, he will do so without your aid or mine."[22] This account allegedly proves that Calvinism kills mission. God is sovereign, so He will convert people when He wants to; therefore, mission is unnecessary.

First, the story about John Ryland and William Carey may be apocryphal. John Ryland's son later denied that the event happened and insisted that his father was not even present at the meeting where he reportedly made these comments.[23] Second, even if Ryland did make these comments, there is not necessarily a direct relationship between any belief in the doctrines of grace and this sentiment. In fact, Michael Haykin has argued that Ryland's statement had everything to do with his doctrine of the end times and nothing to do with his doctrine

---

22. The most recent recounting of this story that I've encountered is in Lois Tverberg, *Walking in the Dust of Rabbi Jesus: How the Jewish Words of Jesus Can Change Your Life* (Grand Rapids: Zondervan, 2012), 132.

23. "The popular story is repudiated by Ryland's son, John Ryland, Jr., who was Carey's close friend and a fellow member of the Northampton Association, being assistant minister at his father's church at the time when the incident was supposed to have happened. 'I never heard of it till I saw it in print, and cannot give credit to it at all.' Among the reasons he gives for rejecting its authenticity, it is interesting to note that he says, 'No man prayed and preached about the *latter-day glory* more than my father.'" Iain Murray, *The Puritan Hope: Revival and the Interpretation of Prophecy* (Edinburgh: Banner of Truth, 1971), 280. Murray cites as source John Ryland, *Life of Andrew Fuller* (London, 1816), 175. For further confirmation, see W. A. Jarrel, *Baptist Church Perpetuity: Or the Continuous Existence of Baptist Churches* (Dallas, 1894), 417. Jarrel quotes Ryland's son as insisting that his father was not even present at the Northampton meeting.

of salvation.[24] Finally, it must be pointed out that William Carey held to the Calvinistic doctrines of grace and saw no conflict between those doctrines and his desire to spread the gospel all over the world. Despite these points, authors continue to appeal to Ryland's outburst to justify their belief that Calvinism spells the death of mission.

To refute this claim, we can appeal to the Reformed confessions, especially to the Canons of Dort. The election described in these confessions is realized in history through means. The hearing of God's word preached is an instrument that the Holy Spirit uses to gather in God's elect. That preaching is done by men, both in established congregations and on mission fields at home and abroad. Reformed churches have always recognized that God's decree of election implies a human responsibility both inside our churches and outside. That recognition is made explicit in our confessional heritage.

For instance, the Canons of Dort state precisely the nature of the means God uses to draw in the elect:

> But when God accomplishes his good pleasure in the elect, or works in them true conversion, he not only causes the gospel to be externally preached to them, and powerfully illuminates their minds by his Holy Spirit, that they may rightly understand and discern the things of the Spirit of God, but by the efficacy of

---

24. Michael A. G. Haykin, "John Collett Ryland and His Supposed Hyper-Calvinism Revisited," *Historia ecclesiastica* (blog), October 9, 2007, http://www.andrewfullercenter.org/blog/2007/10/jonh-collett-ryland-his-supposed-hyper-calvinism-revisited/.

the same regenerating Spirit he pervades the inner-most recesses of the man; he opens the closed and softens the hardened heart, and circumcises that which was uncircumcised; infuses new qualities into the will, which though heretofore dead, he quick-ens; from being evil, disobedient, and refractory, he renders it good, obedient, and pliable; actuates and strengthens it, that, like a good tree, it may bring forth the fruits of good actions. (3/4.11)

How does God call the elect? Reformed churches confess that it is through the preaching of the gospel and the efficacious working of the Holy Spirit in the hearts of human beings. This doctrine does not hinder the work of mission, but powerfully energizes it. Through the preach-ing of men the elect will be gathered in. Therefore, the gospel must be preached by men! Where the gospel is faithfully proclaimed, we can have confidence that God will be working to draw in those who are His, assert the Canons:

This purpose proceeding from everlasting love towards the elect, has, from the beginning of the world to this day, been powerfully accomplished, and will, henceforward, still continue to be accomplished, notwithstanding all the ineffectual opposition of the gates of hell; so that the elect in due time may be gathered into one, and that there never may be want-ing a Church composed of believers, the foundation of which is laid in the blood of Christ, which may steadfastly love and faithfully serve Him as their Savior, who, as a bridegroom for His bride, laid down His life for them upon the cross; and which may celebrate His praises here and through all eternity. (2.9)

This means that our fundamental attitude with regard to mission can always be positive. Even when the mission work of the church does not appear successful from a human perspective, God's purposes will never be frustrated. Whether through one missionary or another, whether through one sermon or another, through whatever means He chooses, God will gather His elect. Therefore, we can submit in hope to God's sovereignty with the firm assurance that the gates of hell will never prevail over His church-gathering work. The Canons of Dort, therefore, powerfully remind us not only of our missionary responsibility but also of our missionary confidence.

In view of all of this, we can give thanks to God for this well-formulated and biblical part of our Reformed confessional heritage. The Canons of Dort have stood the test of time. They have served us well as a fortress, protecting the church against false teaching. But they have equally served as a weapon for the tearing down of strongholds that exalt proud people in the place of God. As they carry out their missionary responsibility, our Reformed churches can only benefit more by giving increased attention to this latter function. By doing so, the result will be more glory for the sovereign God who saves by His grace alone.

Conclusion

The Reformation was a movement back to the Bible. In many important ways, the pre-Reformation church had departed from Scripture. The Reformers intended to bring the church back to the Word of God as the only foundation. Consequently, one of the pillars of the Protestant Reformation was the well-known Latin expression *sola Scriptura*.

Sola Scriptura, however, in no way precluded the development of Reformed confessions. Having Scripture alone as the church's standard did not rule out the production of confessional statements, which aimed to identify and summarize the important teachings of Scripture. On the contrary, in a period of instability and confusion, confessions were seen as absolutely imperative. For example, the followers of the papal church too easily were inclined to group all Protestants with violent, revolutionary Anabaptists. Confessional statements such as the Belgic Confession made the case that the Reformed churches were different because they respected and embraced the full gamut of biblical teaching.

In both their origin and essence, the Three Forms of Unity, like all Reformed confessions, have an outward orientation. Confessions have an inward orientation as well. They express the biblical faith that unites believers in our Reformed churches, and they are used as teaching tools within our churches. These confessions are the plumb line for the teaching of Reformed office bearers in our churches. However, it is also the case that these documents exist to *proclaim to the world* the faith revealed in Scripture. We place these documents on our church websites, for example, so that when the curious visit and ask what we believe, they can find a ready answer. These confessions are not the church engaged in conversation with itself, but the church testifying to the nations what the Scriptures hold forth as being of the greatest importance.

Since they have an inherent missionary value, it is no surprise that, as we have seen in the preceding chapters, Reformed missionaries continue to use them to great effect. Around the world, in vastly different cultures, the Three Forms of Unity are still being employed to spread the biblical good news and to establish true churches of Jesus Christ. The missionary versatility of these confessions should not be underestimated. While they remain culturally conditioned to a certain extent, they have still managed to transcend cultural barriers. From Ukraine to the Philippines to Brazil and many places in between, these Reformed confessions continue to powerfully serve the cause of missions.

Because they are a faithful summary of Scripture's most important teachings, the Three Forms of Unity also remind the church of her missionary calling and provide some resources for reflection on that calling. These confessions speak of the call to "win our neighbors for Christ" and show how the Lord will graciously work through our efforts to draw in the elect and fulfill His purposes in this world. While we acknowledge that they are not comprehensive in their missiological scope, we have seen in this brief volume that there is far more than is often recognized.

The Three Forms of Unity are a rich repository of biblical truths, a precious heritage given to us by the Lord. In an age of rampant anticonfessionalism, the challenge falls to us to still see this treasure for what it is, lovingly embrace it, and steadfastly maintain it. The challenge is ours not only to continue holding forth this inheritance to an unbelieving world as a testimony for the gospel but also to further explore the ways in which it speaks to the church's missionary task. True, the Scriptures first of all call us to have a heart for this lost world. However, since the Reformation was a movement back to those Scriptures, we see the same call in the confessions that the Reformation produced. Being faithful, God-glorifying Reformed churches today includes heeding that divine call.

Select Bibliography

Bangs, Carl. *Arminius: A Study in the Dutch Reformation*. Nashville: Abingdon Press, 1971.

Bierma, Lyle D. *An Introduction to the Heidelberg Catechism: Sources, History, and Theology*. Grand Rapids: Baker Academic, 2005.

Boice, James Montgomery, and Philip Graham Ryken. *The Doctrines of Grace: Rediscovering the Evangelical Gospel*. Wheaton, Ill.: Crossway, 2002.

Book of Praise: Anglo-Genevan Psalter. Winnipeg, Man.: Premier Printing, 2010.

Bosch, David. *Transforming Mission: Paradigm Shifts in Theology of Mission*. Maryknoll, N.Y.: Orbis, 1991.

Braekman, E. M. *Guy de Brès, I. Sa Vie*. Brussels: Editions de la Librairie des Eclaireurs Unionistes, 1960.

Braekman, E. M., E. A. De Boer, Ruth Pieterman, and Madeleine Gimpel. *Guido de Bres: zijn leven, zijn belijden*. Utrecht: Kok, 2011.

Bredenhof, Wes. *For the Cause of the Son of God: The Missionary Significance of the Belgic Confession*. Fellsmere, Fla.: Reformation Media & Press, 2011.

———. "John Calvin and Missions." *Christian Renewal* 27, no. 11 (February 25, 2009): 24–27.

———. "The Other Confession of Guido de Brès." *Clarion* 60, no. 22 (October 21, 2011): 526–27.

————, ed. *We Believe: The Creeds and Confessions of the Canadian Reformed Churches*. Hamilton, Ont.: Providence Press, 2010.

Calvin, John. *Institutes of the Christian Religion*. Edited by John T. McNeill. Translated by Ford Lewis Battles. 2 vols. Philadelphia: Westminster Press, 1960.

Collinet, Robert. *La Réformation en Belgique au XVIme Siècle*. Brussels: Editions de la Librairie des Eclaireurs Unionistes, 1958.

De Brès, Guy. *Confession de foy, faicte d'un commun accord par les fideles qui conversent ès pays bas*. Rouen: Abel Clemence, 1561.

————. *Le baston de la foy chrestienne*. Geneva: Nicolas Barbier & Courtreau, 1558.

De Bujanda, J. M. *Thésaurus de la littérature interdite au XVIe siècle: Auteurs, ouvrages, editions*. Vol. 10 of Index des livres interdits. Geneva: Librairie Droz, 1996.

De Jong, P. Y. "The Dawn of a New Day." In *Secession, Doleantie, and Union: 1834–1892*, by Hendrik Bouma, 237–54. Neerlandia, Alta.: Inheritance Publications, 1995.

Den Boer, William. *God's Twofold Love: The Theology of Jacob Arminius (1559–1609)*. Göttingen: Vandenhoeck & Ruprecht, 2010.

Dennison, James T. Jr., ed. *1523–1552*. Vol. 1 of *Reformed Confessions of the 16th and 17th Centuries in English Translation*. Grand Rapids: Reformation Heritage Books, 2008.

————. *1552–1566*. Vol. 2 of *Reformed Confessions of the 16th and 17th Centuries in English Translation*. Grand Rapids: Reformation Heritage Books, 2008.

Faber, J. *Vestigium Ecclesiae: De doop als spoor der kerk (Cyprianus, Optatus, Augustin)*. Goes: Oosterbaan & Le Cointre N.V., 1969.

Godfrey, W. Robert. "Popular and Catholic: The *Modus Docendi* of the Canons of Dordt." In *Revisiting the Synod of Dort (1618–19)*, edited by Aza Goudriaan and Fred van Lieburg, 243–60. Leiden: Brill, 2011.

———. "Tensions within International Calvinism: The Debate on the Atonement at the Synod of Dort, 1618–19." PhD diss., Stanford University, 1974.

Gootjes, Nicolaas. *The Belgic Confession: Its History and Sources.* Grand Rapids: Baker Academic, 2007.

———. *Teaching and Preaching the Word: Studies in Dogmatics and Homiletics.* Winnipeg, Man.: Premier Publishing, 2010.

Heck, Sebastian, and Jon Payne, eds. *A Faith Worth Teaching: The Heidelberg Catechism's Enduring Heritage* (Grand Rapids: Reformation Heritage Books, 2013).

Helleman, Adrian A. "The Heidelberg Catechism and Missions." *The Banner* 119, no. 32 (September 10, 1984): 6–7.

Hendrix, Scott H. *Recultivating the Vineyard: The Reformation Agendas of Christianization.* Louisville: Westminster John Knox Press, 2004.

Hoekema, Anthony A. "The Missionary Focus of the Canons of Dort." *Calvin Theological Journal* 7, no. 2 (November 1972): 209–20.

Horton, Michael. *The Christian Faith: A Systematic Theology for Pilgrims on the Way.* Grand Rapids: Zondervan, 2011.

Hyde, Daniel R. *With Heart and Mouth: An Exposition of the Belgic Confession.* Grandville, Mich.: Reformed Fellowship Inc., 2008.

Janssen, R. C. *By This Our Subscription: Confessional Subscription in the Dutch Reformed Tradition Since 1816.* Kampen: Theologische Universiteit, 2009.

Kaajan, H. *De Groote Synode van Dordrecht in 1618–1619.* Amsterdam: N. V. De Standaard, 1918.

Keizer, G. *De afscheiding van 1834: haar aanleiding, naar authentieke brieven en bescheiden beschreven.* Kampen: J. H. Kok, 1934.

Klooster, Fred H. "Missions—The Heidelberg Catechism and Calvin." *Calvin Theological Journal* 7, no. 2 (November 1972): 181–208.

———. *Our Only Comfort: A Comprehensive Commentary on the Heidelberg Catechism.* 2 vols. Grand Rapids: Faith Alive Christian Resources, 2001.

Kuyper, H. H. *De Post-Acta of Nahandelingen van de Nationale Synode van Dordrecht in 1618 en 1619 gehouden....* Amsterdam: Hoveker & Wormser, 1899.

Lombard, Peter. *The Sentences.* Books 1–4. Toronto: Institute of Medieval Studies, 2007–2010.

Luther, Martin. *Luther's Works.* Saint Louis: Concordia Publishing House, 1958– .

Meijerink, H. J. "The Origins of the Canons of Dort." In *The Bride's Treasure: Introduction to the Canons of Dort,* by J. Faber, H. J. Meijerink, C. Trimp, and G. Zomer, 1–37. Launceston, Tasmania: Publication Organisation of the Free Reformed Churches of Australia, 1979.

Monter, William. "Heresy Executions in Reformation Europe, 1520–1565." In *Tolerance and Intolerance in the European Reformation,* edited by Ole Peter Grell and Bob Scribner, 48–64. Cambridge: Cambridge University Press, 1996.

Moreau, A. Scott, Gary R. Corwin, and Gary B. McGee. *Introducing World Missions: A Biblical, Historical and Practical Survey.* Grand Rapids: Baker, 2004.

Muller, Richard A. *God, Creation, and Providence in the Thought of Jacob Arminius: Sources and Directions of Scholastic Protestantism in the Era of Early Orthodoxy.* Grand Rapids: Baker, 1991.

———. *The Unaccommodated Calvin: Studies in the Foundation of a Theological Tradition*. New York: Oxford University Press, 2000.

Murray, Iain. *The Puritan Hope: Revival and the Interpretation of Prophecy*. Edinburgh: Banner of Truth, 1971.

Neill, Stephen. *A History of Christian Missions*. New York: Penguin, 1964.

Pettegree, Andrew. *Reformation and the Culture of Persuasion*. Cambridge: Cambridge University Press, 2005.

Plass, Ewald M., comp. *What Luther Says: An Anthology*. 3 volumes. Saint Louis: Concordia Publishing House, 1959.

Praamsma, Louis. "The Background of the Arminian Controversy (1586–1618)." In *Crisis in the Reformed Churches: Essays in Commemoration of the Great Synod of Dort, 1618–1619*, edited by Peter Y. De Jong, 39–56. 1968. Reprint, Wyoming, Mich.: Reformed Fellowship, 2008.

Richards, George W. *The Heidelberg Catechism: Historical and Doctrinal Studies*. Philadelphia: Publication and Sunday School Board of the Reformed Church in the United States, 1913.

Schalkwijk, F. L. *The Reformed Church in Dutch Brazil (1630–1654)*. Zoetermeer: Uitgeverij Boekencentrum, 1998.

Schutte, Kevin Allen. "The Missional Church and New Church Development in the CRCNA." MA thesis, Calvin Theological Seminary, 2003.

Sinnema, Donald. "The Drafting of the Canons of Dordt: A Preliminary Survey of Early Drafts and Related Documents." In *Revisiting the Synod of Dort (1618–19)*, edited by Aza Goudriaan and Fred van Lieburg, 291–333. Leiden: Brill, 2011.

———. "The Issue of Reprobation at the Synod of Dort (1618–1619) in Light of the History of This Doctrine." PhD diss., University of St. Michael's College, Toronto, 1985.

———. "The Origin of the Form of Subscription in the Dutch Reformed Tradition." *Calvin Theological Journal* 42, no. 2 (November 2007): 256–82.

"Smalcald Articles (1537)." In *Concordia: The Lutheran Confessions*, 259–85. 2nd ed. Saint Louis: Concordia Publishing House, 2005.

Stranglin, Keith D., and Thomas H. McCall. *Jacob Arminius: Theologian of Grace.* Oxford: Oxford University Press, 2012.

Steinmetz, David. "The Scholastic Calvin." In *Protestant Scholasticism: Essays in Reassessment,* edited by Carl Trueman and R. Scott Clark, 16–30. Carlisle, Pa.: Paternoster Press, 1999.

Tennent, Timothy C. *Invitation to World Missions: A Trinitarian Missiology for the Twenty-First Century.* Grand Rapids: Kregel, 2010.

The Constitution of the Reformed Dutch Church in the United States of America. New York: William Durell, 1793.

Tucker, Ruth A. *From Jerusalem to Irian Jaya: A Biographical History of Christian Missions.* Grand Rapids: Academie Books, 1983.

Ursinus, Zacharias. *The Commentary of Dr. Zacharias Ursinus on the Heidelberg Catechism.* Translated by G. W. Williard. Reprint, Phillipsburg, N.J.: P&R, 1985.

Van't Spijker, Willem. "'Den Hals Buygende Onder Het Jock Jesu Christi…' Oorsprong en zin van een uitdrukking in art. 28 en 29 van de Nederlandse Geloofsbelijdenis." In *Bezield Verband: Opstellen aangeboden aan prof. J. Kamphuis,* edited by J. Douma, 206–19. Kampen: Van den Berg, 1984.

———, ed. *The Church's Book of Comfort.* Grand Rapids: Reformation Heritage Books, 2009.

Van't Spijker, W., C. C. de Bruin, H. Florijn, A. Moerkerken, and H. Natzijl. *De Synode van Dordrecht in 1618 en 1619*. Houten: Den Hartog, 1987.

Van Asselt, W. J. *Introduction to Reformed Scholasticism*. Grand Rapids: Reformation Heritage Books, 2011.

Van Halsema, Thea B. *Glorious Heretic: The Story of Guido de Brès*. Grand Rapids: Eerdmans, 1961.

Van Reken, Calvin. "The Mission of a Local Church." *Calvin Theological Journal* 32, no. 2 (November 1997): 344–67.

Van Rongen, G. *The Church: Its Unity in Confession and History*. Neerlandia, Alta.: Inheritance Publications, 1998.

Walls, Andrew. *The Missionary Movement in Christian History: Studies in the Transmission of Faith*. Maryknoll, N.Y.: Orbis, 1996.

Warfield, B. B. "The First Question of the Westminster Shorter Catechism." *Princeton Theological Review* 6, no. 4 (October 1908): 565–87.

———. "What Is Calvinism?" In vol. 1 of *Selected Shorter Writings of Benjamin B. Warfield*, edited by John E. Meeter, 389–92. Reprint, Phillipsburg, N.J.: Presbyterian and Reformed Publishing Co., 1970).

Scripture Index

Confessions Index